Wilson and
Revolutions:
1913-1921

Lloyd C. Gardner

Rutgers University

The America's Alternatives Series

Edited by Harold M. Hyman

Wilson and Revolutions: 1913-1921

J. B. Lippincott Company

Philadelphia/New York/San Jose/Toronto

ISBN 0-397-47348-6
Library of Congress Catalog Card Number 75-31983
Printed in the United States of America

1 3 5 7 9 8 6 4 2

Library of Congress Cataloging in Publication Data

Gardner, Lloyd C.   1934-
    Wilson and revolutions, 1913-1921.

    (The America's alternatives series)
    Bibliography: p. 145
    1. United States—Foreign relations—1913-1921.
2. Russia—History—Allied intervention, 1918-1920.
3. United States—Foreign relations—1913-1921—
Sources. 4. Russia—History—Allied intervention,
1918-1920—Sources. I. Title.
E768.G34   327.73   75-31983
ISBN 0-397-47348-6

Contents

v

Foreword ═══════════════════════════

"When you judge decisions, you have to judge them in the light of what there was available to do it," noted Secretary of State George C. Marshall to the Senate Committees on the Armed Services and Foreign Relations in May 1951.[1] In this spirit, each volume in the "America's Alternatives" series examines the past for insights which History—perhaps only History—is pecularly fitted to offer. In each volume the author seeks to learn why decision makers in crucial public policy or, more rarely, private choice situations adopted a course and rejected others. Within this context of choices, the author may ask what influence then-existing expert opinion, administrative structures, and budgetary factors exerted in shaping decisions? What weights did constitutions or traditions have? What did men hope for or fear? On what information did they base their decisions? Once a decision was made, how was the decision-maker able to enforce it? What attitudes prevailed toward nationality, race, region, religion, or sex, and how did these attitudes modify results?

We freely ask such questions of the events of our time. This "America's Alternatives" volume transfers appropriate versions of such queries to the past.

In examining those elements that were a part of a crucial historical decision, the author has refrained from making judgments based upon attitudes, information, or values that were not current at the time the decision was made. Instead, as much as possible he or she has explored the past in terms of data and prejudices known to persons contemporary to the event.

1. U.S., Senate, Hearings Before the Committees on the Armed Services and the Foreign Relations of the United States, *The Military Situation in the Far East,* 82d Cong., 2d sess., part I, p. 382. Professor Ernest R. May's "Alternatives" volume directed me to this source and quotation.

Nevertheless, the following reconstruction of one of America's major alternative choices speaks implicitly and frequently, explicitly to present concerns.

In form, this volume consists of a narrative and analytical historical essay (Part One), within which the author has identified by use of headnotes (i.e., Alternative 1, etc.) the choices which he believes were actually before the decision makers with whom he is concerned.

Part Two of this volume contains, in whole or part, the most appropriate source documents that illustrate the Part One Alternatives. The Part Two Documents and Part One essay are keyed for convenient learning use (i.e., the Alternative 1 reference in Part One will direct readers to references to appropriate Part Two Documents). The volume's Part Three offers the user further guidance in the form of a Bibliographic Essay.

Presidents' reactions to revoluntionary movements abroad affected our domestic and foreign policies from the first years of American national history. But not since those early years when the French Revolution swirled around all nations, was a president so concerned with revolution as was true of Woodrow Wilson. His perceptions of the swift social, political, and ideological changes taking place, first in nearby Mexico, then in distant Russia, and his derivative policy options for America, opened the way to the unquiet present.

Professor Lloyd Gardner has reconstructed major aspects of the compelling story of Wilson's responses to revolutions in a revealing manner. From close examination of Professor Gardner's restatement and analysis, and of the accompanying documents, readers are able to travel far along the policy roads Wilson and his close counsellors discerned. Judgments concerning the wisdom and timeliness of decisions made fifty years ago, in the light of attitudes and information then available, may help to illuminate the many paths that have led us to our bicentennial position in the world.

Harold M. Hyman
Rice University

Part One

Wilson and Revolutions

1

Petrograd and Washington: November, 1917

At two o'clock on the morning of November 7, 1917, small bands of armed workers and sailors slipped out of hiding onto the streets of Petrograd. Each group, led by political advisers known as "commissars," had been assigned a specific target: a railroad station, the lighting plant, the waterworks, the telegraph station, the state bank. By ten o'clock in the morning all were taken and secured. A few hours later startled foreign journalists heard one of the revolutionary leaders tell an emergency session of the Petrograd Soviet that the Provisional Government had ceased to be. "We do not know of a single casualty."

The announcement was a bit premature. The Winter Palace, seat of the Provisional Government, offered some resistance and did not surrender for another twelve hours. But the ease with which the Bolsheviks carried out the capture of Petrograd revealed that the Provisional Government was a corpse waiting to be buried by anyone bold enough to say so out loud—and then do it. Few thought the Bolsheviks would last very long either. They claimed adherence to the thought of a German philosopher (or was it economist?), a man named Karl Marx, and they were supposed to be against private property. "Have you heard about it?," someone shouted along the Nevsky Prospect, a main street of the Russian capital. "The Bolsheviks have seized the power. Well, that won't last more than three days. Ha ha ha!" [1]

Ten months later the Bolsheviks still held power. But they had had to fight to retain it, and a civil war was beginning that would last for three years. During those months the new regime in Russia had become a major preoccupation of Allied statesmen. In Washington, President Woodrow Wilson brooded about his duty toward Russia. He wrote his close friend and adviser, Colonel Edward M. House, that he had been sweating blood over the Russian question, asking himself what was right and what was feasible. It turned to pieces like quicksilver under his touch, he complained.

Pressure on Wilson to "do something" about Russia had increased steadily. He was told that the Bolsheviks, led by Vladimir I. Lenin, were nothing more than German agents, or, if not actually agents, disreputable men who had no scruples about delivering their country over to the Central Powers. Others warned the president that he had a moral obligation to aid Russian "liberals" against the Bolshevik tyranny. Visitors to the White House leaned forward in their chairs to whisper to the president that the greatest danger was that bolshevism would spread across Europe—even to America—unless steps were taken to halt its advance within Russia.

3

Left alone, Wilson had to weigh these claims and other factors against his public commitment and private conviction in defense of the right of national self-determination. How could any intervention be squared with such a basic principle? On the other hand, did a revolutionary government have an absolute right to exist if it endangered the prospects of military victory over Germany, and the stability of postwar Europe? It was a wrenching decision for the president, and one he could not avoid making. Having asserted a strong claim to moral leadership among the Allies, it was up to him to confront the Bolshevik challenge. And because America's material power was greater than that of the exhausted Allies, the president's decision would set the limits of any intervention in Russia. His was the moral obligation to choose, and the power to accomplish the end—if it was to be done at all.

President Wilson had greeted the overthrow of Russian tsardom with warm enthusiasm. The revolution of March, 1917, had brought into being a Provisional Government, which was immediately heralded as a good omen in the struggle against German autocracy. The March revolution purified the Allied cause just as Wilson was considering what he must do about Germany's decision to resume unrestricted submarine warfare.

The tsar's fall had a different impact in European capitals. Some welcomed it, but many more expressed concern about Russia's ability to stay in the war. They knew it was important for the American president to be able to speak of a clash between good and evil in persuading his own people to go to war, but did he know what dangers were ahead in Russia, and what would happen if the new government dropped out of the war? It was hard to say what Wilson believed, except that his war message to Congress cited the Russian Revolution as additional proof that America was joining and taking command of a crusade not simply to defeat Germany and its cohorts, but to establish a permanent alliance among democratic nations to prevent future wars.

The worst fears of Allied statesmen were all too soon realized. The collapse of the Provisional Government brought into power men who openly wished for the destruction of the old order, and any new order based on capitalism and nationalism. Perhaps it could be said that the European Allies were the most concerned about the preservation of the old order, and American leaders about the securing of the new. Never mind, the Bolsheviks despised both. American war aims, jeered the Bolsheviks, were but the latest product off the capitalist assembly line, shabby delusions glossed in Wilsonian rhetoric to fool the workers. Wilson's professed "liberalism" would not end the war. Only the workers could do that, because only the workers could take power from the capitalist ruling class—the men who had made this war and who would make the next one. Imperialism was not a state of mind, as Wilson persisted in believing; it was not a matter of good and bad nations, as capitalist leaders pretended; it was the logical result of class rule and manipulation of national governments.

The war against the Central Powers was a struggle for land and material resources, but the Bolshevik challenge represented the struggle for men's minds as well. For Wilson it combined a personal and an ideological challenge.

At stake was everything: the fruits of military victory over Germany, including the League of Nations, and (as Wilson well knew) America's image before the world and its vision of itself. It is in this context that alternatives for dealing with the Bolshevik problem were presented and acted upon or ignored. Each alternative had a historical dimension; each posited a definition of the future. To choose one today narrowed tomorrow's options, not simply in Russia, but everywhere. No one understood this better than the historian who sat up late at night in the White House turning over the probable consequences of the actions urged on him.

Wilson's Alternatives

Wilson's quest for a world made safe for democracy, already complicated by the secret treaties among the Allies, was dealt a severe blow by the Bolshevik triumph. It had been generally agreed in the United States by the end of the neutrality period (1914-1917) that in the future a great power must do more than merely insist upon its rights under international law. Another world conflict like the present one would sweep away international law, and with it the foundations of what serious men called western civilization. Hence the only way America could preserve its future would be to preserve the world's future. Where men disagreed was on the question of how this was to be accomplished. Wilson's view had many supporters, but just as many or more in America and Europe still trusted in arms and alliances.

A liberal-democratic Russia could have played a significant—if not crucial—role in determining which way the matter was settled. At least Wilson thought so, as did a number of his advisers. Standing beside America at the peace conference, Russia, the newest democracy, would have lent powerful support to the president's insistence that the treaty must reflect a concern with justice—not revenge. Together Russia and the United States could have curbed the ambitions of powers and men who looked to the past, and guided the world safely into the future.

The important point here was not that Wilson had worked all this out to such detail—he had not—but to suggest how much more difficult the Russian situation made things for him in his dealings with the other nations at Versailles. Following this argument in a somewhat different direction, the president could perhaps persuade himself (or be persuaded by others) that if he could not lead the Allies *with* Russia's help, it might be necessary to lead them *in* Russia. Put yet another way, Wilson might conclude that he could not allow the Allies to dominate the Russian situation, just as he could not allow German domination.

At the time of the Bolshevik revolution the Allies and the Central Powers had been at war more than three years. Both sides were near exhaustion. The Russian revolutions of 1917 were symptomatic of that exhaustion, a warning to national leaders in each alliance that if the war did not end soon the people might take matters into their own hands. American intervention was supposed to change stalemate into Allied victory. But would it? Was there time enough if Russian troops abandoned the frontlines and returned home to get their share of the bread and land Lenin promised them instead of the starvation and death they faced in the trenches? If that happened, the war could end with Germany in control of Eastern Europe militarily and dominant economically in Russia. Such an outcome would almost certainly deprive the Allies of victory, and deny Wilson his League of Nations. Extreme bitterness against any Russian government which would desert either cause was only natural—and the Bolsheviks seemed determined to do just that.

In some ways the Bolshevik program crisscrossed Wilsonian themes; and wherever it did the result was confusion, making the president's tasks on the ideological front just that much more difficult. Wilson's commitment to national self-determination, for example, was greater than that of his allies. Not surprisingly, the men who governed Europe had to be concerned with strategic frontiers. Outside their own continent, moreover, they ruled over vast colonial empires; even the most enlightened among them were hardly prepared to turn over their colonies to native rulers. European conservatives respected the Monroe Doctrine. They expected equal consideration when it came to restoring and preserving order in their neighborhoods.

How much difference was there, then, between "extreme" Wilsonians and Bolsheviks on the colonial question? It was a matter of some urgency for the president's supporters and for his opponents. Wilson wanted to work with liberal elements within the Allied countries, but he could not afford to antagonize moderates and conservatives by allowing his program to be stolen by the radical left and used for their own purposes. Wilson's defense of self-determination was already in danger of being lost to Leninism, as the Russian leader asked for and received support from left-liberal circles in the West who agreed that Russia must be left to determine its own fate. Lenin could blend Marxist rhetoric into Wilsonian themes, when and if it suited him, to turn the tables on those who urged intervention against the Bolsheviks by challenging their right to rule in Africa and Asia. He could, so to speak, ideologically counter-intervene in the colonial world.

Such expedient behavior by Lenin and the socialist left in other countries put terrific pressure on the liberal alliance behind Wilson. He and his supporters found they could not challenge the restoration of the old order in Europe (minus a powerful Germany) without sounding pro-Bolshevik. Isolated between revolution and reaction, the embattled Wilsonians faced an unhappy choice. As a result they temporized to save their position, and saw their numbers dwindle as the struggle became a contest between conservative indignation and liberal expectation. Victory over the Central Powers actually made things worse in this regard. In Europe, the elimination of Germany meant that a unifying factor among the Allies was gone. They were free to resume pursuit of national self-interest and less dependent upon the good will of the United States. On both sides of the Atlantic the end of the war meant that the problems of reconstruction and readjustment had to be faced. Fear of bolshevism grew in proportion to the difficulties of industrial reorganization, producing the "red scare" throughout the capitalist world.

American conservatives soon came to see the rise of domestic radicalism as yet another result of Mr. Wilson's war. There were also fears that, one way or another, the Bolshevik revolution would drag the nation back into some new fool's errand overseas. Already the Japanese were using a version of the red scare to justify what they had always wanted to do in Siberia. And the French were doing the same in Eastern Europe.

Wilson shared these suspicions. Opposed to Bolshevism from his innermost being, he had nevertheless suspected Allied motives from the first hints that they had decided upon proposing military intervention as a solution. Little wonder he sweat blood trying to decide what to do about Russia. To state the options before Wilson is, of course, to reduce the complexity of historical reality to suit our convenience. It seems clear that Wilson resolved against direct dealings with Lenin, but beyond that one principle were no fixed alternatives, as daily choices strengthened or modified the *direction* of American policy. If Wilson could have counted on Congressional support for his decisions, for example, how might that have changed his position? As historians usually see it, Wilson gave consideration to the implications of three alternatives in making his decisions about revoluntionary Russia, and acted accordingly:

Alternative 1: HE COULD HAVE DECIDED TO APPROACH LENIN IN A SERIOUS EFFORT TO ESTABLISH FORMAL RELATIONS. Theoretically this choice was open to Wilson any time from November, 1917, until March, 1921, when he left office. Practically speaking, however, it was a real option only until the decision in July, 1918, to send troops to Siberia. At no time did Wilson move in this direction. A Bolshevik rebuff would have strengthened his hand in some quarters, but Wilson was more concerned that Lenin might take advantage of such an offer to advance the revolutionary cause. The other side of this option, of course, was that recognition would mean taking sides in the civil war and abandoning Russian "liberals" to their fate—and possibly the cause of liberalism generally to radicals and reactionaries.

Alternative 2: HE COULD HAVE GONE "ALL-OUT" TO PREVENT THE BOLSHEVIKS FROM ESTABLISHING THEMSELVES BY MILITARY ACTION. This choice was never a practical option if only because Congress would not have supported the president. Certainly the Allies had no chance alone of "restoring order in Russia." The temptation to intervene—if only to speed up the inevitable failure of the Bolsheviks—was hard to resist. Wilson yielded to it by sending troops to Siberia and offering some measure of support to the English and French interventions in European Russia. He always argued, however, that American participation in these ventures was not part of a concerted effort to drive Lenin from power by military action, but to preserve the true Russian revolution from alien domination. He insisted that an all-out offensive would end in allowing the Bolsheviks to draw upon the resources of Russian nationalism to defeat their opponents.

Alternative 3: THAT LEFT WILSON A POLICY OF "WATCHFUL WAITING." First attempted in regard to the Mexican Revolution, "watchful waiting" combined nonrecognition with other pressures (both positive and negative) to achieve (or preserve) a "constitutional" revolution. It seemed to him the only way to deal with men who had lost their senses and taken a nation with them. Eventually, it was fervently hoped, this time of troubles would come to an end: then the true Russian spirit would emerge to claim what had been stolen from the people by the hated Bolsheviks. When that happened, the Russian nation would thank the American people, the only ones who had not sought to profit from their temporary plight.

The distinctions between Alternatives 2 and 3 did not always impress Wilson's critics, both left and right, however much the president insisted upon them. A similar problem had existed earlier when Wilson drew a sharp moral distinction between German submarine warfare and the Allied blockade, and justified going to war on that basis. In private he would always add reasons of state to those of morality, but Wilson was unconvincing as a realist. He opposed Bolshevism, in the final analysis, as he had opposed German autocracy: because they endangered democracy. But that still leaves a crucial question: how did Wilson define democracy?

Notes

1. Quoted in Leon Trotsky, *The History of the Russian Revolution* (3 vols., Ann Arbor, Michigan: The University of Michigan Press, 1957), III, 236.

2

Options for a Liberal: Woodrow Wilson's Creed

The process that brought Woodrow Wilson to these options in dealing with Russia—and face to face with his own assumptions—began during the Civil War era. The "second American Revolution," as the war was called by the most famous historian of the Progressive era, Charles Austin Beard, had special significance for Wilson, a Southerner with firsthand experience of what revolutionary violence did to a traditional society. Reared in a clerical home, Wilson also absorbed the lessons of his forefathers' strict Calvinism. He fused these experiences into a righteous liberalism. Southern Presbyterianism made harsh demands, but it gave the believer added strength of will to persevere in the face of adversity.

It produced in Wilson a liberal creed, but it had also turned out stalwart conservatives such as John Caldwell Calhoun, the austere and able spokesman for Southern sectionalism. Wilson and Calhoun shared the same heritage—and perhaps the same temperament—but they were separated by the Civil War, the dividing line between sectionalism and nationalism, between an unbending defense of peculiar institutions and the search for a new national identity. Wilson fought the so-called Bourbon reconstructionists, Calhoun's political heirs, insisting that the "new" South would have to find its way back by becoming more national in outlook than the "special interests" which now dominated political life in the North and which controlled the Republican party.

If the South had anything to give the nation, said Wilson standing Calhoun's logic on its head, it was the re-affirmation of the country's early faith in its Constitution, and the evolution of its institutions in a world endangered by reaction and revolution. The Civil War and Reconstruction had demonstrated that military force (Alterative 2) was not likely to bring about the desired results. Neither, thought Wilson, would the radical "Populist" program save the South. An address prepared for the centennial of George Washington's inauguration on April 20, 1889, demonstrated that Wilson, then a professor of history at Wesleyan University, had already reached some tentative conclusions about all revolutions and revolutionaries:

> For us this is the centennial year of Washington's inauguration; but for Europe it is the centennial year of the French Revolution. One hundred years ago we gained, and Europe lost, self-command, self-possession. But since then we have been steadily receiving in our

9

midst and to full participation in our national life the very people whom their home politics have familiarized with revolution: our own equable blood we have suffered to receive into it the most feverish bloods of the restless old world. We are facing an ever-increasing difficulty of self-possession with ever deteriorating materials: for your only reliable stuff in this strain of politics is Character.[1]

Wilson's "youthful" declamation against Europe radicalism (and its infiltration into American life) was no more harsh than his denunciation of Populist efforts to take over the Democratic party fifteen years later (see Document 1). In each instance his complaint was that revolution offered no answer to the just grievances of the disadvantaged. Thus the future president's experiences with the aftermath of "revolution" in the South and the "new immigration" in the North had already produced a strong aversion to dealing directly with radicals of any sort. And this long-held conviction no doubt played some part in Wilson's firm rejection of any diplomatic approach to Lenin's government.

With both Bourbons and Populists, on the other hand, Wilson shared the view that the Civil War and Reconstruction had been about tariffs and railroads as much or more than concern with emancipation of the slaves. Northern "imperialism" against the South dominated historical and popular interpretations of the Civil War era in Wilson's time. D.W. Griffith's famous film epic, *Birth of a Nation*, which appeared in 1913 (the year Wilson entered the White House), stressed the mistakes Radical Republicans had made in attempting to restructure the South by turning it over to ignorant blacks incapable of self-government—let alone managing the affairs of state governments. Near anarchy had been the result. The new nation could not really be born, the film asserted in so many reels, until the North gave up the effort to coerce the South.

Charles and Mary Beard's *Rise of American Civilization*, published in the next decade, gave a more authoritative stamp of approval to the commonly held thesis that even the Fourteenth Amendment, supposedly designed to protect the rights of the freedmen of the South, had actually been drawn up to protect capitalist corporations. Southern suspicions of "capitalists" and "bankers" had at last been vindicated! From Jefferson through Jackson to Woodrow Wilson, Southern liberals identified their opponents as the "special interest" men of the North. This explains Wilson's lifelong suspicion of New York bankers, his steady low-tariff views, his opposition to Theodore Roosevelt's New Nationalism as no more than state-supported corporation rule, and his traditional opposition to Republican desegregation policies in the federal government as pandering to the black vote to insure the party's continued control of the nation.

If his fear of revolutionaries led Wilson to reject direct dealings with the Populists or later with the Bolsheviks, his equally deep distrust of "special interests" drew him to the cause of the poor whites of the South and the "submerged masses" of foreign countries. In foreign policy, especially, Wilson as president convinced himself on several critical issues that he was being thwarted by the special interests of foreign nations. One example was the influence he believed British oil companies exercised on their government's policy towards Mexico. Indeed, in this instance he finally concluded that foreign oil companies (and their allies) constituted the major stumbling block to the emergence of a liberal national government in Mexico.

Yet Wilson could also say with full conviction that the Anglo-Saxon people had undertaken to reconstruct the affairs of the world, and could not withdraw their hand without betraying their best instincts. How were the Anglo-Saxon people to accomplish this task, one wonders, without using the capitalist institutions they had developed at home to do it? Wilson had an answer. His solution rested on certain assumptions about character and history.

The Jefferson Heritage

Jefferson was an ardent expansionist, but opposed colonial empire. So was, and so did, Woodrow Wilson. Empire put a limit on man's imagination, reduced his capacity to develop free institutions, and was the presumed antithesis of everything American. Yet Jefferson imposed colonial rule on the Louisiana territory, and Wilson intervened in Mexico. How explain such contradictions? In both instances the answer was that the President expected to exercise these broad powers only to teach the peoples of those areas to elect good men to office. Jefferson succeeded; Wilson did not. One reason was that it had become more difficult to export the American revolution in the twentieth century, but Wilson had the harder task under any circumstances. Jefferson only had to deal with a population already under colonial rule; Wilson faced a nation in revolution.

But there were other problems connected with trying to adapt Jefferson's revolutionary views to the modern world. It was axiomatic in Jefferson's time that freedom of ideas and freedom of goods must be equated. Shut off the one, and the other must suffer. It was possible to be anti-capitalist and pro-free trade in that era, and thus did Jefferson protest against British maritime politics: "If any nation whatever has a right to shut up to our produce all the ports of the earth, except her own, and those of her friends, she may shut up these also, and so confine us within our own limits."[2] There is in this passage, written in 1793, the beginning of another powerful strain in American thought: that their revolution must carry free goods and free ideas to the end of the earth, or see them disappear at home. The limits Jefferson feared most were not territorial and economic, but ideological.

The difficulty Americans felt, their sense of insecurity in a world dominated by European empires, was genuine enough. They were confronted at every turn, and in every marketplace, by mercantilist power and theory. According to the latter, colonies had no right to trade with anyone except the mother country. Free trade was a weapon against tyranny in the early nineteenth century. But a century later Wilson and many of his fellow countrymen still saw the world and the internatiolnal economic struggle in much the same terms.

While special relationships still existed between colonies and the metropolitan nations of Europe, the American revolution had succeeded. Revolutions in this century were directed at another set of problems, ones not amenable to the solutions of Jefferson's time. There was bound to be a confrontation between these worldviews, but in Wilson's campaign for the presidency the issue was still high tariffs and monopolies, and the need to produce a New Freedom for all Americans. Perhaps the most significant vote cast in 1912, from this point of view, was that for Eugene Debs, the Socialist candidate, which totaled nearly a million, more than twice as many as in 1908.

Throughout the campaign Wilson stressed the same theme, often using the same figure of speech. American industries, he repeated again and again, had expanded to such a point that they were about to "burst their jackets" unless new outlets were found. "There is nothing in which I am more interested," he told delegates to the 1914 National Foreign Trade Convention, "that the fullest development of the trade of this country and its righteous conquest of foreign markets."[3]

The New Freedom Versus Revolution

As president, Wilson moved at once to clear away tariff obstructions to increased foreign trade and competition at home. Congress responded by passing the first significant reduction of the protective tariff since the Civil War. Wilson's ambassador to Great Britain was delighted, explaining that future textbooks would mark the occasion as the moment when commercial supremacy passed from Europe to the United States. Wilson fully agreed, but he was too busy for self-congratulations. In addition to tariff legislation, Wilson extracted from Congress new banking regulations which permitted American banks to establish overseas branches. This act, promised Secretary of State William Jennings Bryan, would do more to promote foreign trade than any other congressional measure in the nation's history. A third measure to provide ship subsidies to carry the goods to foreign markets eluded the president until the nation went to war in 1917.

Meanwhile new problems had arisen. A few weeks before Woodrow Wilson entered the White House, an aide advised him of rumors concerning impending revolutions in the hemisphere. According to these stories certain revolutionary-minded adventurers, who had been held in check during the years of Republican rule, were convinced that the Democrats would not come chasing after them with a "big stick" if they misbehaved. Wilson brought the matter before an early cabinet meeting. He had been informed, the President began, that there were agitators all primed to set off revolutions in various countries. He did not intend to let them get away with it.

Wilson then produced the statement he and Secretary Bryan had drafted (see Document 2) as a warning to anyone contemplating such action. The formula made some sense in regard to revolutionary activity then common practice in the Caribbean area and the smaller "banana" republics of Central America. An unhappy fact of life in these countries was the presence of a cadre of unscrupulous would-be petty tyrants whose all-consuming interest was to secure power long enough to fill their pockets with customs receipts or foreign loans. To get this money, moreover, these unenlightened "caudillos" would cheerfully bargain away their countries' rights and natural resources to the highest bidder.

Politics in these countries was often a matter of "ins" and "outs," with the winners declared by who could muster the strongest army—or, occasionally, by foreign interference. It was this latter possibility which disturbed the American State Department. There was the Panama Canal to think about, but the United States had always looked upon the growth of European interests in this region as part of a worldwide struggle with "imperialism." Between 1875 and 1900, the colonial powers, instead of declining, had reached out to grasp huge new areas. China and Latin America remained the two most important noncolonial areas on the globe. United States policymakers wanted to see these underdeveloped places stay part of the "free world" of that day. They were just as serious about this as later officials were in stating a determination to halt communist expansion.

In 1898 the United States had won a battle in this ongoing struggle when Cuba and the Philippines were "liberated" as a result of the Spanish-American War. Roosevelt and Taft had established a system of American protectorates in the Caribbean, but Wilson and Bryan seemed to want to try something else, more in line with American democratic traditions. Bryan's idea was to issue a summons to revolutionary leaders, asking them to attend formal conferences. At these meetings they were to select one of their number to act as a provisional president pending American-supervised elections. The man thus chosen would serve out his term in safety, backed by American power and, if Bryan had his way, economic support. Through this process these countries would soon become liberal democracies—or enough like them to solve the problem.

Haiti proved obstinate, offering instead economic concessions if the United States would leave island politics alone. Bryan was appalled, and delivered a sharp rebuff to the authors of this unthinkable proposal:

> While we desire to encourage in every proper way American investments in Haiti, we believe that this can be better done by contributing to stability and order than by favoring special concessions to Americans. American capital will gladly avail itself of business opportunities in Haiti when assured of peace and quiet necessary for profitable production.[4]

For more than two years the secretary of state was unable to pin down any Haitian government long enough to put into operation his version of what would later be called "welfare imperialism." In 1915 he finally recommended, and Wilson approved, military intervention. Significantly, the administration retained its anticolonial purity by justifying the action as an act of self-defense against the danger of French or German occupation. Yet the original plan predated the war, and American troops stayed in Haiti until 1933.

Despite this conspicuous failure in the Caribbean, where the president's antirevolutionary manifesto had some relevance to actual conditions, the method for establishing democratic governments by summoning a convention of revolutionary leaders was given a second chance in the administration's policy toward the Mexican Revolution, and yet a third chance when Wilson confronted the Bolsheviks. It did not work any better in those two situations.

Watchful Waiting in Mexico

Wilson inherited several revolutionary problems from his predecessors. He was called upon to decide about recognition of the new Chinese Republic early in his first term. It was an easy decision for Wilson, who saw the Chinese Revolution of 1911 as a long step forward toward a Chinese democracy, and toward the elimination of parasitic foreign interests which had gained the upper hand in the last days of the Manchu Dynasty. Consistent with this attitude, he refused to support American participation with foreign bankers in an international consortium for loans to China. As Wilson put it, to have continued participation in such a combine would have sacrificed America's moral position *in* China and would have constituted an unnatural restraint on trade *with* China (see Document 3).

Wilson was also asked to decide about recognition of a new government in Mexico, headed by General Victoriano Huerta. This was a much tougher decision. For more than half a century Mexico had been ruled by a dictator, Porfirio Diaz, who governed with the aid and support of a powerful elite. Diaz had sought to balance off European and American investors offering each large concessions in the hope that neither group became too powerful within Mexico. But the old man finally lost in 1910, the result of a combination of factors including a new national spirit within the conservative elite and general dissatisfaction among the peasant classes. These were the basic ingredients of a revolutionary situation with strong anti-American overtones.

Diaz's successor, Francisco I. Madero, promised political and economic reforms. He was too radical for conservatives, and much too conservative for peasant leaders like Emiliano Zapata and Pancho Villa. On top of this, Madero seemed to lack any real talent for administration. President Taft had a deep foreboding about the Mexican situation: he had prayed that Diaz would last until he left the White House. Most of William Howard Taft's prayers went unanswered; Mexico was no exception. Madero's inability to restore order led President Taft, albeit reluctantly, to send the fleet into the Gulf of Mexico. Meanwhile, private financiers (with the encouragement of the State Department) sought to persuade Mexican authorities to accept large loans as an alternative to new taxes and excessively nationalistic reforms. But even Mexican conservatives had become wary of relying upon foreign capital to develop their country's resources. Legislation to regulate the mining industry had been introduced—and passed—while Diaz was still in power.

The American Ambassador, Henry Lane Wilson, made no secret of his contempt for Madero. Ambassador Wilson was a more adventurous man than President Taft. He was prepared to take risks to restore the *ancien régime*.

Given the welter of armed revolutionary and counterrevolutionary forces vying for power in Mexico, it is difficult to assess his influence in Madero's fall. But the ambassador did play a direct role in determining his successor.

Early in 1913 Madero faced an onslaught led by Felix Diaz, nephew of the old dictator. The turning point came when Victoriano Huerta—one of Madero's own generals—betrayed his trust and went over to the other side. At a meeting in the United States embassy, Huerta and Diaz made a compact: the general was to become provisional president, and, at the proper time, support Diaz's candidacy for a regular term. Ambassador Wilson presided over these doings like a colonial high commissioner, though he had no mandate to do so from Washington. This discrepancy proved to be a source of confusion and discomfort for European diplomats.

These events transpired at the very end of the Taft administration, in January and February of 1913. While refusing to grant Huerta immediate diplomatic recognition, Taft advised the British ambassador that he saw nothing in the Mexican situation that might lead him to depart from an announced policy of nonintervention. It was a cautious statement to be sure, but the ambassador also reported that president-elect Woodrow Wilson could be expected to take the same view. Meanwhile, however, rumors were spreading throughout the diplomatic community that Ambassador Henry Lane Wilson was deeply involved in the assasination of Madero by Huerta's secret agents. While this story troubled some European representatives, it seemed clear to them that the American ambassador, as doyen of the diplomatic corps in Mexico City, had been acting in the interests of Mexican stability in securing an agreement between Huerta and Diaz, and that Washington was, if not pleased about methods, satisfied with the results. Surely it would only be a matter of time until diplomatic recognition was granted, and business as usual resumed.

Wilson discussed the issue at early cabinet meetings, but no decision was reached. Someone suggested that Mexico had become a battleground of rival British and American oil interests. A general conviction prevailed in the cabinet that Huerta's action constituted a backward step for the hemisphere, but no decision was taken to apply the president's March 11, 1913, circular on Central American revolutions directly to Mexico. Outside the cabinet, Wilson's close friend and adviser, Colonel Edward M. House, advised the president to wait and see whether Huerta abided by his promise to step aside in favor of Felix Diaz.

The president and his advisers felt that if the United States extended diplomatic recognition to Huerta it would seem to be condoning the action of militarists and reactionaries not only in Mexico but wherever else such "revolutions" took place. Even at this early date the Mexican issue was seen as having general significance for the conduct of American foreign policy. Convinced that the State Department was unduly influenced by years of Republican domination in the executive branch, and that its representatives abroad were all "Dollar Diplomats" without much scruple, Wilson sent his own investigators into Mexico. Their reports further persuaded him that

General Huerta was no more than a usurper. Radical agrarian leaders and even moderate "constitutionalists" like Venustiano Carranza would never accept him.

Wilson's explanation for his refusal to grant diplomatic recognition left European listeners cold and suspicious. To make it stick, moreover, Wilson had to come up with a definition of diplomatic recognition as moral acceptance of a foreign government instead of simple acknowledgement of its existence. This distinction between *de facto* recognition and *de jure* recognition became an issue not only in Mexico, but later when Wilson applied it to the Bolsheviks. It has left a lasting imprint on American diplomacy, and is in itself one source of an interventionist policy since it requires the wielder to make a positive case for the morality of any new government.

Europeans argued that American recognition would open up to Huerta the outside support he needed to defeat the rebels, the money to stabilize Mexican finances and to purchase whatever arms Mexican soldiers required. If the American president refused to allow Huerta this aid, therefore, it must be because he had it in mind to destroy European interests in Mexico, leaving a clear field for Americans. The only trouble with that deduction was that American capitalists with large interests in Mexico actively opposed the president's policy.

Months went by without any hint that Wilson would intervene either for or against Huerta. What was Wilson waiting for? In November the British sent a special ambassador to find out. Wilson was reassuring: "I beg that you will assure Sir Edward Grey [British Foreign Minister] that the United States Government intends not merely to force Huerta from power but also to exert every influence it can exert to secure for Mexico a better government under which all contracts and business and concessions will be safer than they were."[5] American consuls had been instructed to impress on those in authority in Mexico City as well as the rebel chiefs that foreign property must be protected.

Grey was relieved to hear this, but things got worse—much worse. American opposition finally brought about Huerta's retirement, but not before American ships had shelled the Mexican Naval Academy in Vera Cruz and landed an occupying force. A second Mexican-American War seemed not unlikely in April, 1914. If conflict should come, the president told Congress, it would be only against "General Huerta and those who adhere to him," not against the Mexican people. Here was still another precedent for American policy in the Russian Revolution. Wilson was saved from a war decision in 1914 by Huerta's realization that between opposition from rebel forces in his own country and pressure from America he could not long remain in power. The general left Mexico—on a British ship.

The symbolism was perfect, but, unfortunately, reality did not live up to it. Wilson quickly sent special representatives to each of the rival anti-Huerta leaders urging them to get together to settle on one of their number for the presidency. He asked each to give a pledge that would allow for an orderly democratic solution to Mexican problems. Ironically, Wilson's intervention against Huerta made it less likely that he could influence any of the dictator's erstwhile opponents. Huerta had very nearly succeeded in making Wilson and the United States a scapegoat for his own failings. Anti-Americanism was at a high pitch after the Vera Cruz incident. No Mexican leader could have conceded so much to Wilson and still hoped to control the various elements of the revolution.

For a time the president settled on Pancho Villa as the most likely man to lead Mexico along approved paths into the modern world. Of all the rivals for Mexican leadership, Villa was the *least* likely choice for such a task. He was a modern Robin Hood perhaps, but not a Simon de Bolivar. Wilson's most determined effort to get a firm grasp on the Mexican Revolution, however, came in approaches to Venustiano Carranza. A wealthy landowner, Carranza seemed an almost equally unlikely candidate to fill Madero's shoes. But he was the leader of the "Constitutionalist" faction, and Wilson thought that was a good omen. If it was, it was not a favorable sign for American investors in Mexico. What made Carranza a revolutionary was his nationalism. Since control of Mexico's natural resources by and for Mexicans was a patriotic issue, the two went together naturally. This phenomenon appears in many revolutionary situations when some conservatives choose nationalism with radicalism in preference to foreign control. It would show up in both Russia and China in the following decades.

It can be argued that nationalism predominated over radicalism in the 1917 Constitution Carranza promulgated, but to American leaders concerned with the worldwide emergence of a revolutionary threat to capitalism it came as an unpleasant shock. According to Article 27 of the new Mexican Constitution, ownership of subsoil natural resources was vested in the central government. Aliens could own land or exploit mineral resources only if they agreed in advance not to call upon their home governments in disputes with Mexican authorities. It was certainly a radical measure in comparison with similar documents governing the rights and limitations of private property in more "advanced" countries. Efforts were made to portray Carranza as influenced by supposed German sympathies—or filled to the brim with Bolshevik sentiments.

Wilson did not know what to do. He had resisted appeals for intervention by his new secretary of state, Robert Lansing, but he seemed unable to leave the Mexicans alone. Meanwhile, American and British oil companies paid "protection" money to local adventurers who promised to shield them against other marauders and against the legal enforcement of Mexican law. At one point Wilson declared that every country "had a right to struggle after liberty in whatever way it liked . . . a country was free to set its own home on fire if it chose, and in that case other people did well to come away from the flames" The President did not, however, follow his own advice.

Mexico had come to represent for the Wilsonians the results of the "robber baron" era, an unhappy land dominated by special interests—the same selfish forces Wilson had vowed to bring under control at home. But this vision had difficulty adjusting to and accommodating the Mexican solution Carranza promulgated in the constitution of 1917. This document, it appeared to concerned Americans, was the product of a more extreme form of agrarian radicalism than Populism, but still the same sort of phenomenon Wilson had opposed. This tension made it difficult for the president to decide upon any course of action. When America entered the war, the Mexican Revolution was pushed into the background, but no one forgot about it or failed to see the possible connection between events in Petrograd and Mexico City. And where else? (*Alternative 3:* See Document 4).

In both Mexico and Russia, finally, Wilson had started out fighting counter-revolution, and ended struggling to contain and control the very forces he had unknowingly encouraged by condemning reactionary special interests and imperialism.

Notes

1. Address on the One Hundredth Anniversary of the Inauguration of George Washington, in Ray Stannard Baker and William E. Dodd eds., *The Public Papers of Woodrow Wilson*, 6 vols. (New York: Harper & Bros., 1925-1927), I, 184-85.

2. Cited in Lloyd C. Gardner and William L. O'Neill, *Looking Backward: A Reintroduction to American History* (New York: McGraw-Hill, 1974), pp. 88-89.

3. Cited in Martin J. Sklar, "Woodrow Wilson and the Political Economy of Modern United States Liberalism," in Ronald Radosh and Murray Rothbard, eds., *A New History of Leviathan* (New York: E.P. Dutton & Co., 1972), p. 33.

4. Bryan to Thomas Bailly-Blanchard, December 19, 1914, in U.S., Department of State, *Papers Relating to the Foreign Relations of the United States, 1914* (Washington, D.C.: Government Printing Office, 1922), pp. 370-71.

5. Cited in Arthur S. Link, *Wilson: The New Freedom* (Princeton: Princeton University Press, 1956), pp. 376-77.

3

America and Russia Before the Fall

American relations with Russia since the turn of the century had been almost nonexistent—by choice. A few policy makers and businessmen had argued for closer contacts, but Americans looking at Russia usually saw only an Asian rival. In the Russo-Japanese War (1904-1905), Washington made no effort to conceal its fondness for the brave little men who had challenged the Russian bear—and thereby preserved American interests as well. Even those who suspected Japan's ultimate motives in Asia did not therefore conclude that one remedy would be to seek an understanding with St. Petersburg. Tsarist Russia was the least understood of all European countries; and what Americans did know about that strange land did not appeal to them. At the outset of the war in 1914, Colonel House had expressed his opinion that if the Allies won, it would mean Russian domination of the Continent, and if Germany won, it would mean the tyranny of militarism for generations to come.

Indeed, the thought of German hegemony giving way to Russian overlordship was an early stimulus to the president's desire to replace the old balance of power order with a League of Nations. As the war went on, however, Russia came to share in the general sympathy Americans bestowed on the suffering Allies. For more practical reasons than sympathy, it was decided that the time had come to negotiate a new commercial treaty with Russia, an earlier one having lapsed as a result of American displeasure at the tsar's policies in general and specifically the infamous anti-Jewish repressions known as pogroms. Allied war orders had fostered a new prosperity in the United States, but many worried about what would happen in the long run. As things stood, Russian purchases were handled through British purchasing agents; after the war this trade would slip back into British hands unless the United States had in the meantime taken steps to establish itself on a permanent footing in the Russian market.

The man selected by the Wilson administration to negotiate the new commercial treaty with Russia was David R. Francis, a former Democratic governor of Missouri who lacked any knowledge of the land or its language. He was considered a skillful commercial negotiator, however, one who would not be taken in by any smooth talk from America's business rivals. Francis was particularly concerned, as were his superiors in Washington, that England and France would manage to tie up Russia in a system of mutual preferences for the postwar period which would deny American as well as German access to Russian trade and investment (see document 5). The ambassador's struggle to prevent that continued over the next several months—right up to the March Revolution. Wilson had formulated a reply to the Anglo-French danger in the course of several prewar speeches in which he set forth the principles of equal access to world trade and raw materials and open covenants of peace.

As in Jefferson's day, and for the same reasons, the desire to open trade relations with new-found allies had many dimensions. While it was thought necessary to counterbalance Allied plans in Russia to prevent London and Paris from controlling that nation's postwar trade, for example, it was of equal importance to prevent the spread of a system so at odds with American liberal principles. The primacy of narrow "economic" motives over other considerations was not an issue. And in times of revolution and war, the policy maker simply does what he can to prevent his future options from being foreclosed.

The momentuous events in Russia seemed to portend, for a brief time, that the world was moving steadily toward American principles, and away from those of old Europe. The United States recognized (and welcomed) the Provisional Government on March 22, 1917, two full days before England and France acted. Ambassador Francis was delighted. He had pleaded for immediate recognition, urging Washington to be first in greeting a government which, he said, fulfilled every criterion for a democracy. Like Huerta, Tsar Nicholas had been banished. By being the first to welcome "democratic" Russia to the community of nations, the United States gained a significant moral advantage over its European partners. At the same time, however, it acquired a material responsibility for the survival of the Provisional Government. Wilson eagerly grasped the former; he and his aides had a more complicated task in finding the means to satisfy the latter.

In his war message of April 2, 1917, the president proclaimed the new Russia "a fit partner for a league of honor" (see Document 6). The next day Secretary of State Lansing cabled Ambassador Francis that he was to ascertain if financial aid was desired by the Russian government. The ambassador lost no time in recommending a large loan: "Russia owns boundless forests, immeasurable deposits of ores and oil, and immense areas of tillable lands. This loan in my judgment would be absolutely safe. Furthermore it is advisable from every viewpoint of policy."[1] Lansing then stated American conditions for such aid: would Russia be able—and determined—to carry on the war if a loan were forthcoming? Again Francis was confident: he had warned top officials that no aid would be extended if a separate peace were concluded with Germany. The minister of finance had assured him in reply, "there is no possibility" of a separate peace.

It took some additional time to clear away bureaucratic obstacles, but on May 17, 1917, Francis was informed that a $100,000,000 loan had been authorized for the Provisional Government. On July 14, $75,000,000 more was put at its disposal; in August another $100,000,000, and in October a final $50,000,000 was granted. Only a portion of this money was ever actually used by the Provisional Government, and compared to previous British and French loans the total of American aid was a drop in a very large bucket. In addition to Anglo-French wartime aid, these two nations had invested and loaned billions of dollars in prewar Russia. Before the war began all the big power stations in Russia were in foreign hands. Ninety percent of the joint stock of Russia's mining industry was foreign-owned. English and French capital had built the railways, developed the coal of the Ukraine and the oil of the Caucasus.

If Russia left the war, therefore, America's hope for the future would be badly damaged, as Francis put it, "from every viewpoint of policy." But worse damage would be done to the Allied stake in the present if Germany appropriated for itself the riches of Eastern Europe. Not only would the Allies stand to lose their investments, but the war itself. With Russia out of the war, Germany could resupply itself from the most fertile areas of Eastern Europe, defy the Allied blockade indefinitely, and remain the dominant power on the Continent.

Against a background of continuing instability in Russia, Allied and American representatives met to consider the situation confronting the Provisional Government in carrying on the war. It was agreed that every sacrifice should be made to retain Russia in the Alliance and to infuse into her the energy necessary to hold out at all costs. England was assigned responsibility for rehabilitation of the Russian navy; France was to attend to the army. The United States undertook the reorganization of the Russian transportation system, especially the railways.

Caught in the Middle: Kerensky's Dilemma

To the Progressive mind there could not have been, under ordinary circumstances, a more congenial task for America than the rationalization of the Russian transport network. A commission had, in fact, been sent to Russia in May, headed by John F. Stevens, a railway expert who had been involved in the early planning and construction of the Panama Canal and in locating the Great Northern Railway across the Rocky Mountains. If anyone could untangle the snarls on the Trans-Siberian Railway, Stevens would have seemed perfect for the job. American interest in the Trans-Siberian and other Asian lines antedated the war by some years. In 1909, for example, Secretary of State Philander Knox had proposed to the powers, including Russia, the "neutralization" of Manchurian railroads as a venture in international cooperation for the economic development of a key Far Eastern area.

The March revolution seemed to many a perfect opportunity to accomplish several goals at once. The American ambassador to Great Britain cabled Washington on March 31, 1917, that American management of the Trans-Siberian Railway would greatly help the Russian military situation and prove an invaluable key to postwar industrial development. Washington agreed on both counts. The Stevens Mission had little time to accomplish anything while the Provisional Government remained in power, but it became a crucial element in Wilson's "watchful waiting" for the Bolsheviks to fail—by keeping Siberia "neutralized" as long as possible.

Meanwhile, the administration had supplemented economic credits and the railroad mission with an ideological offensive in Russia. Wilson despatched a special mission to Russia under the leadership of former Secretary of State Elihu Root, a staunch conservative, who was used to paying $1,000 per month for housing in prewar Washington. What he knew about revolutions and revolutionaries—and what he felt about those he did know of—hardly qualified him for such delicate work. He was balanced, however, by representatives from "all walks of American life," including the elderly vice-president of the American Federation of Labor, James Duncan, and even a Socialist of the nonrevolutionary type, Charles Edward Russell. No American radicals were asked to go to Russia.

Though the Provisional Government was threatened by the Maximalists (Bolsheviks), the members of the Root mission felt the greatest danger stemmed from German intrigue. They recommended a special advertising campaign to combat German propaganda, headed by "an expert American advertising man with a good assistant" (see Document 7). As a result of the Root mission, special representatives of the Committee for Public Information (CPI) were sent to Russia to explain American war aims and Russia's stake in their achievement. Only by defeating Germany, said CPI men, could Russia preserve the gains it had made in the March revolution.

Not everyone associated with the Root mission agreed with this diagnosis of Russia's ills, nor with the recommended cure. Secretary of State Lansing had become deeply pessimistic, writing in his private diary on August 8, 1917, that the Russian Revolution would in all likelihood pass through the usual cycle: "First, Moderation. Second, Terrorism. Third, Revolt against the New Tyranny and restoration of order by arbitrary military power."[2] America, he added, should await its opportunity to act until the third stage. But Lansing's views were not Wilson's. In the president's mind, Russia was still seen "to have been always in fact democratic at heart" (see Documents 8 and 9).

Whatever the Provisional Government was at heart, it was not competent to deal with the current crisis without substantial aid and sympathy from America and the Allies. Even with such aid and understanding, its survival was in doubt from the beginning. The March revolution had come as a direct result of labor strikes and bread riots. Behind those disturbances were three years of war during which Russia had suffered 9 million casualties, including 1.7 million dead and 4.9 million wounded. The remaining casualties were the result of disease. Under the strains of war, the tsarist bureaucracy had all but collapsed. Sir George Buchanan, the British ambassador, tried to warn the tsar of what was happening outside the palace early in 1917, but only succeeded in drawing from Nicholas II a pathetic defense of absolute monarchy from a bygone era.

The tsar had even become separated from members of the ruling elite, in part because of the influence of Rasputin the Monk on the royal family. Rasputin virtually controlled the tsarina by virtue of his supposed ability to "cure" her son's hemophilia through hypnosis. The tsarina, it was said bitterly, ruled her husband. So who ruled Russia? Upper-class faith in the monarch—if not in the monarchy—was rapidly being undermined. In a last desperate effort to save Nicholas from his wife's follies, and from himself, a clique of aristocrats murdered the tsarina's beloved "man of God" in December of 1916.

When this stage was reached in the England of Charles I and the France of Louis XVI, upper and middle classes joined in fear and ambition to produce bourgeois revolutions. But in Russia the middle class was a poor, stunted thing, which had never developed economically or politically to a point where it could take over and organize (let alone sustain) a parliamentary revolution on the English or French pattern. It had had its one chance during the abortive revolution of 1905, when the tsar had been forced to summon a Duma. For the first time Russia had an elective legislative body. Nicholas promised that in the future no law could obtain force without the consent of the State Duma. As soon as the threat diminished, however, the tsar retracted, announcing new Fundamental Laws which proclaimed him once again the supreme autocrat, and under which he could resume complete control of the armed forces, foreign affairs, and all the executive branches of government.

The Duma's failure to establish its independence and authority vis-a-vis the throne stemmed in part from fear of working-class movements. For several months a St. Petersburg "Soviet" had challenged all political authority in Russia with a series of strikes. Better to have tsarism (even absolute tsarism perhaps) than anarchy. Conservatives in the Duma rejoiced when the tsar's police arrested the entire membership of the Soviet, though by doing so they reduced their own voice in managing Russia's future. In part, however, the Duma's lack of success in curbing the tsar's dangerous excesses was the product of foreign "intervention"—a point not lost on the Bolsheviks when they came to power. The tsar could not have made his Fundamental Laws stick without outside financial support. This he obtained from French bankers, who also feared the Russian working class and trusted Tsar Nicholas more than their Russian bourgeois counterparts. In April, 1906, the bankers granted Europe's last absolute monarch a loan of $400,000,000. It was the largest loan in the history of mankind, boasted the tsar's prime minister.

By mid-summer 1917, French and English statesmen were desperately trying to make up for a decade-old mistake by pledging all-out support to Alexander Kerensky, the new leader of the Provisional Government. Kerensky had seized power within the Provisional Government on August 7, 1917, as the result of dissatisfaction within the army and navy and a series of protests against Russia's continuing participation in the war. There was not much time left to save "democratic" Russia. But an American diplomat in Russia professed to see a silver lining on the lowering clouds hanging over St. Petersburg: Kerensky had officially branded the Maximalists as German agents in orders to the army and the fleet, he reported. Even more encouraging was his decision to bring to justice all Bolsheviks among the ship crews who were active in a recent mutiny.

Allied leaders wanted Kerensky to do even more in this direction. He was an orator, recalled British Prime Minister David Lloyd George in later years, a master of the eloquence that stirs masses, but he trusted too much to his remarkable gifts, ignoring the fact that there would come a time when he must translate words into action. Lloyd George (and others in positions of responsibility) failed to see, or refused to recognize, that Kerensky could not move effectively against the extreme left or the extreme right without slipping off the high wire. Moreover, the only action he could have taken to stave off the Bolsheviks—a separate peace—was sure to have lost him the support of England and France.

Faced with Allied threats to cut off support if he even faltered in prosecuting the war, dependent upon conservatives who refused to countenance even the slightest abandonment of Russia's territorial war aims, Kerensky soon found himself in an impossible position. By 1916 over a million and a half men had been listed as deserters from the army. This ominous sign was followed in 1917 by an outright revolt among Russian soldiers fighting in France. These men, numbering about fifteen thousand, had been sent to France to be armed and equipped. While there they took part in the spring offensive of that year, and nearly six thousand were killed or wounded. The survivors revolted against French authority, and issued a manifesto denouncing the Allies and the war. On a small scale what happened in France was an exact replica of the general dissatisfaction inside Russia with the Allies.

The French could deal with such mutinies summarily; Kerensky could not deal with his people in the same fashion. Already in revolt against tsarist repression, the Russian citizenry expected an improvement in their condition, not more promises or threats. And for all of their advice to Kerensky, the Allies themselves were prepared to risk very little to help Russia if it meant endangering their own domestic peace. In England, for example, the cabinet was divided over whether to grant Nicholas exile in the British Isles. King George V feared stirring up labor troubles in his realm if he extended an invitation to his royal cousin, so the question was dropped.

Thus the authority of the Duma grew weaker, and the power of the Soviets increased. Kerensky asked the Duma to postpone action on agrarian reform, so the peasants took it upon themselves to partition the great estates. The vital forces of the revolution were sweeping past him—and past those who clung to him as the last hope for Russia. "All Power to the Soviets," demanded the Bolsheviks. The lesson of history, for the Bolsheviks, was that the revolution of 1905 had failed because of the weakness of the bourgeoisie. The revolution of 1917 would fail, too, unless it "grew" into a socialist one.

Lenin Triumphs

It was Lenin who explained the full meaning of this lesson to his fellow Bolsheviks. Not all Bolsheviks had seen this "truth", a major departure from previous doctrine which postulated two revolutions separated by several years. Lenin converted them with speeches and articles. Ambassador Francis was aware of Lenin's arrival on the scene in late April, 1917, but easily dismissed him in a few sentences of a longer report on loan negotiations. An extreme socialist or anarchist named Lenin was making violent speeches, he reported, but his actions were only serving to strengthen the government, which was purposely giving him leeway. Lenin was to be deported at an opportune moment. The moment never arrived.

Lenin's return from exile marked a point of no return for the revolution. Climbing atop an armored car at the Finland station where he arrived, Lenin called out to a huge crowd of many thousands, "Long live the Socialist world revolution!" He had been seventeen years old when he first told friends that he intended to become a professional revolutionary. It was in the same year, 1887, that his brother had been executed for plotting against the life of Tsar Alexander III. His brother's death made a deep impression on the young student, beyond the personal tragedy he felt what also impressed him was his brother's political mistake: terrorism was not revolutionary, Marxism was. In 1893, Lenin joined a group of Marxist intellectuals and made his first serious contacts with workers' groups in St. Petersburg. For these activities and political writings, he was arrested and exiled to Siberia. Upon his release in 1900, he went into a different kind of exile by moving to Switzerland where he established the Marxist journal *Iskra* (The Spark). In 1903 a congress of Russian Marxists split over the question of party organization. Lenin took leadership in the faction called Bolsheviks. Their opponents, the Mensheviks, wanted the party to behave like Western political organizations, open to casual adherents who would vote for party candidates for office.

Lenin heaped scorn on the Mensheviks. A party based on an appeal to the electorate was for "professors and university students," those who could never submit to the discipline necessary for successful underground work. The Bolsheviks, he asserted, must construct an organization of dedicated members, small in number, who were agreed on fundamental objectives and who were prepared to work actively for their achievement. Lenin's presentation fortified orthodox Marxists against their so-called revisionist opponents, who had gained a strong foothold among Western socialists. Revisionists held that socialism could be achieved by electoral methods, and that revolution (like war) was no longer inevitable or necessary. Lenin's position better suited the realities of Russian politics where liberalism had no historic or social roots. His triumph in 1903 paved the way, although few could see it then, for a much greater victory in 1917. It also set him on a collision path with Woodrow Wilson, though neither had any inkling of that impending confrontation (see Document 10).

Lenin stayed safely in the background during the 1905 revolution, leaving Russia as soon as it was clear that it had failed. Back in Switzerland he applied himself to the study of imperialism. In 1916 he published *Imperialism: The Highest Stage of Capitalism*, a pamphlet which directly assaulted the fundamental assumptions of political liberalism. Lenin denied the existence of "good" and "bad" nations. Germany and America, although soon to be at war with one another, were actually very much alike. Both had arrived at the "threshold of the most complete socialisation of production" in the history of man. But the means of production still remained the property of a few. In Germany and America, presumably, the transition to socialism would be the easiest.

The March revolution in Russia posed a tricky situation for Lenin and his followers. By their own analysis, Russia was not ready for a socialist revolution, but they were not sure what Russia was ready for or what role their party should play. The Germans helped to make up their minds for them. Untroubled by ideological niceties, the Germans had only one purpose in mind: to get Russia out of the war, if not by war, then by revolution. For his part Lenin was happy to accept their offer to send him by sealed railroad car into the melee Russia had become.

From this episode grew the myth that the Bolsheviks were in the pay of the German government. Actually the notion that he could sell the Russian people on this idea had been a key part of Kerensky's campaign against the Left from the beginning. Only the Allies and the Root mission bought the argument, though Russian conservatives (many of whom were pro-German themselves) dearly wanted to discredit the Bolsheviks. Dedicated anti-Bolshevik groups took up the idea and went into the business of fabricating documents proving the existence of a German-Bolshevik conspiracy. Representatives of the Committee for Public Information purchased a full complement and succeeded in smuggling them out of Russia. Known thereafter as the "Sisson Documents," these papers became famous when they were certified as genuine by an independent committee of American scholars and distributed to the public under the imprint of the United States government. President Wilson used them to justify American intervention in Siberia and his refusal to recognize Lenin's government.

Years later the "Sisson Documents" were still cited occasionally by some as the true explanation of the Russian Revolution. Given the deteriorating situation on the Eastern Front, Lenin was indeed risking a lot by promoting revolution. The outcome could have been German domination. Sensitive to what might be charged against him in this regard, the Bolshevik leader had declared in public upon leaving Zurich that he was well aware of German motivations, and of what they hoped to gain by strengthening the antiwar movement in Russia.

Meanwhile, the Germans were not alone in seeking to infiltrate "agents" into the Russian situation. Three days before Lenin arrived, George Plekhanov and a group of Mensheviks traveling under Allied auspices stepped down from a train in the Finland station. A month later more than two hundred emigrants, including several other Menshevik leaders, followed Lenin's route through Germany. These returning exiles, Lenin and Plekhanov along with the rest, found the authority of the Duma already under challenge from the workers' Soviets. The Petrograd Societ had passed a resolution—in the name of the Russian Left—refusing to recognize Russian control of the Dardanelles as in any way essential to the national interest. So the first steps in renouncing further participation in the war had actually been taken before Lenin's arrival. The Germans had determined the timing of Lenin's appearance on the Russian scene, and now the Soviets were determining the role the Bolsheviks would be able to play. Lenin was somewhat in the same position as the French revolutionary figure who had looked out the window at a passing crowd, and then turned to declare that as he was their leader he must hurry up and catch them. Lenin was not slow to grasp the opportunity. Bolshevik strength grew within the Soviets, because the Marxists were the best equipped to take advantage of the discontent. They had obligations to no one except themselves. Resolutions were passed demanding not only that Russia renounce its imperialist war aims, but that the Allies give up theirs as well!

The Provisional Government responded to this pressure in two ways. On the one hand, it tried to convince Anglo-French and American diplomats that a new conference to restate and liberalize war aims had become essential if democracy was to survive in Russia. On the other, the government tried to restore national unity with a military offensive. The result of this effort to move in opposite directions at the same time ended in disaster. Russia's European allies were unwilling to sacrifice what they regarded as essential goals even for the sake of the Provisional Government, while Russia's enemies turned the July offensive into a military rout and pressed a counteroffensive into the Baltic coastlands.

In a desperate move the Provisional Government did attempt to suppress the Bolsheviks, but the economic and military crises only deepened. Finally, in September, there appeared on the Russian horizon the strong man Secretary Lansing had predicted would show up in the person of General L.G. Kornilov, commander in chief of the army. But General Kornilov's uprising failed because Kerensky turned to the only place he could to secure immediate help: the Soviets. Bolshevik Red Guards and workers stopped the trains Kornilov needed to move troops and denied him access to the telegraph system to send his messages. A rightist member of the Provisional Government, Foreign Minister Pavel Milyukov, put it simply and accurately: For a short time the choice lay between Kornilov and Lenin. Driven by instinct, the masses pronounced for Lenin.

Bolshevik prestige gained enormously from the Kornilov affair: they had saved the revolution. Leaders of the non-Bolshevik Left in the Provisional Government began to reassess their position. Deprived of real authority in the cities by the Soviets, ignored by the peasantry which had gone about land reform in its own way by direct action, and deserted by the army, Kerensky's government simply fell apart. Lenin had predicted back in July that he would have to seize power in September or October when the Provisional Government would be too weak to carry on.

So, on the night of November 6, Lenin emerged from hiding around eleven o'clock, caught a street car to the center of Petrograd, and assumed leadership of "his" revolution. Meanwhile movie theaters continued to show their films to large audiences. Lenin had not really seized power but had picked it up from the streets while others continued about their business, amazingly unaware of the great change that had taken place.

Notes

1. Francis to Lansing, April 6, 1917, in U.S., Department of State, *Papers Relating to the Foreign Relations of the United States, 1918, Russia,* 3 vols. (Washington, D.C.: Government Printing Office, 1932), III, 2-3.

2. Diary Entry for August 8, 1917, in, *The Papers of Robert Lansing* (Library of Congress, Washington, D.C.)

4

Ideology and Circumstance: The Bolsheviks in Power

Kerensky left Petrograd to rally loyal forces to fight the Bolsheviks, departing in a car flying the American flag. He never returned. Ambassador Francis's initial reaction to the Bolshevik triumph sounded like a sigh of relief: the worst had come; now things would begin to get better. Lenin could never hope to remain in power, and within a few weeks level-headed men would take charge, and rebuild Russia along democratic lines. The ambassador's detached survey of Russian prospects did not convince many, probably not even himself. On one occasion he greeted an arriving American official grimly with the statement that he would never talk to a "damned Bolshevik." A more balanced estimate came from Consul-General Maddin Summers, who warned his superiors in Washington that the Bolsheviks would urge a separate peace with Germany. To prevent that catastrophe, S mmers recommended the retention of all American agencies in order to lend moral support to the better elements (anti-Bolsheviks) in Russia (see Document 11).

Summers's advice was adopted as a stopgap rationale for maintaining unofficial representation, while denying to any "faction" formal diplomatic recognition. In the meantime, the Bolsheviks had transformed the Second All-Russian Congress of Soviets into an official policymaking body. The congress, now dominated by the Bolsheviks, approved a Council of People's Commissars with Lenin as president, and Leon Trotsky as Commissar for Foreign Affairs. Acting in place of the Duma, the congress unanimously approved two resolutions. The first, the Decree on Land, abolished private ownership of the soil, and the second, the Decree on Peace, called for an immediate opening of peace negotiations.

In the United States Wilson greeted the proposals of the Bolshevik government with incredulity. He inserted a paragraph in remarks he had prepared for the American Federation of Labor Convention then meeting in Buffalo. His slighting reference to the "dreamers in Russia" displayed not a little pique, linking them with pacifists in other countires who wanted peace but could never achieve it by their methods (see Document 12). It was the first indication of Wilson's attitude toward the Bolshevik regime, an attitude that would not change essentially over the next three and a half years he remained in the White House, however much he came to appreciate what had led to the Russian Revolution.

Lenin was a dreamer who had seen his dream materialize, and was now prepared to take whatever steps necessary to protect it from destruction, even when it meant altering traditional Marxist thinking to suit Russian circumstances. The Bolsheviks had expected the European war to be transformed into a class war. If that did not happen, if the soliders and workers *outside* Russia did not now unite against capitalist rulers in other nations, the revolution *inside* Russia would fail. But it would not fail. Not only were the peoples of all countries war-weary, but now the Bolsheviks had in their hands the infamous "secret treaties," the ultimate proof that the masses had been betrayed by their leaders. Publication of these treaties (actually diplomatic correspondence between the Allied governments in which certain territorial promises were exchanged) began on November 23, 1917, in *Izvestia* and continued over the next several days. Translations appeared in the Western press and caused an uproar in Allied capitals—but no revolutions.

Foreign Commissar Trotsky told a colleague that he had accepted the post because it was a small one and he wanted to have more time for party affairs. "My job is a small one: to publish the secret documents and to close the shop."[1] In his autobiography, however, he described his functions at that time with a slightly different emphasis: "I will issue a few revolutionary proclamations to the peoples of the world and then shut up shop."[2] That minor change in emphasis actually revealed a big gap between ideology and circumstance. Apparently it was necessary to give the world revolution a little nudge. Maybe a push? (see Document 13.)

Similarly, while foreign recognition was presumed unimportant in Marxist circles, since the revolution *must* come anyway, Trotsky attempted to cover his bets by warning Allied representatives that so long as recognition was denied his government "we will follow our own course appealing to the peoples. . ." (see Document 14.) On December 26, 1917, this was given practical meaning in a resolution placing two million rubles at the disposal of the commissarat of Foreign Affairs for the needs of the world revolutionary movement. Here was the beginning of what the outside world would later call "Communist subversion." Russian representatives in foreign countries were to be provided with money to distribute for the encouragement and support of local revolutionaries. No secret diplomacy was involved. Convinced that their own survival depended upon the world revolution beginning at once (before the capitalists put aside their petty national differences and turned on the workers' state), the Bolsheviks had absolutely no reason to hide their international activities. In fact, success depended upon the whole world knowing about their "subversive" aims, and acting upon that knowledge.

In addition to money, Trotsky soon started distributing free information. A section for international propaganda was established, whose first project was a German language newspaper issued daily "for free distribution among our German brothers." Similar publications soon appeared in Magyar, Roumanian, Serb, Czech, and Turkish. So while the CPI was attempting to counter Bolshevik propaganda inside Russia, the Bolsheviks were busy launching an ideological offensive of their own. The main effort of Soviet propaganda, however, was directed at the people living under the control of the Central Powers. It was not merely a coincidence that this should be. After all, Germany confronted the new regime with an immediate military threat. So there was, even at this early stage, a distinction to be drawn between capitalist powers. In the circumstances of Soviet power, geography was at least temporarily more important than politics or economics.

The question now became: what would Lenin, the dreamer become realist, make of this distinction? On the other side, what would Wilson, the presumed idealist, make of it? The Bolshevik leaders also drew a distinction between Allied capitalist powers, which posited that Great Britain would remain the most hostile while the United States would become the most interested "in investing its capital in Russia" even under bolshevism (see Document 15.) American leaders made no response to these hints, but maintained unofficial contacts with the new government for fear of driving Lenin into the arms of the Germans, or, as some still supposed, for fear of giving him an excuse to carry out a prearranged plan. Even if the Communists did not last long they could have a lasting effect on the world by turning Russia over to the Germans, or by setting the world afire with revolution.

Decision Against Recognition

A minor direct confrontation with the Bolsheviks had already occurred in Manchuria, where they had made an effort to seize control of the terminus of the Chinese Eastern Railway at Harbin. Russian soldiers and workingmen, acting in sympathy with their comrades in Petrograd, had attempted to overthrow General Horvat's administration of the Russian-owned line. The United States supported Horvat diplomatically and verbally, but shied from encouraging "an armed conflict." The situation resolved itself when the Chinese sent their own troops to occupy Harbin.

American policy makers moved very cautiously in this early crisis, encouraging the Chinese to employ troops to protect their sovereignty and territorial integrity, but staying clear of any direct responsibility for military acts against the Bolsheviks. Harbin was a key point because from that city one could reach out to control the Siberian railway system with a relatively limited number of troops. Control of that network, in turn, might enable the Allies to establish a lifeline to the various centers of anti-Bolshevik activity in the Caucasus region. The United States also had to be concerned about the danger of encouraging, or providing an excuse for, Japanese intervention on the mainland of Asia. Secretary Lansing made it quite clear to the Japanese ambassador that the American government believed that it would be unwise for either nation to send troops to Vladivostok, as it would undoubtedly result in unifying the Russians under the Bolsheviks against foreign interference. The ambassador noted his agreement, but mentioned that England and France had made such a suggestion.

This important conversation in December, 1917, indicates what would become a major constraint on American policy makers in developing alternatives to meet the Bolshevik challenge: military action anywhere would involve the United States in the "secret diplomacy" of the Allies, who had already worked out a "spheres of influence" approach to dealing with the Bolsheviks. The British and the French, for example, had become very interested in General A.M. Kaledin, a cossack leader who had sided with Kornilov and who now raised his anti-Bolshevik banner in the Caucasus to which a number of political exiles and military figures rallied.

Kaledin's movement seemed to offer the possibility of maintaining an Eastern front against the germans, a buffer area between the Bolsheviks and the Balkans, and a political alternative to early recognition of the Soviet regime. Diplomatic recognition of Kaledin was out of the question—at least for the time being— but Anglo-French agents in South Russia were instructed to offer up to ten million pounds to any organized military units prepared to continue Russian resistance to the Central Powers. Kaledin's activities came to Lansing's attention during the second week of December, at a time when a number of issues connected with the Bolshevik Revolution were troubling his mind.

Sending aid to Kaledin might prove to be just the answer, thought the secretary of state, who advised Wilson that he could encourage anti-Bolshevik movements that way and demonstrate "our readiness to give recognition to a government which exhibits strength enough to restore order and a purpose to carry out in good faith Russia's international engagements." (See Document 16). They discussed the plan on the evening of December 11, 1917, and Lansing drafted a message the next day to send to the American representative on the Inter-Allied Council on War Purchases and Finance. Wilson returned the secretary's draft with the brief notation, "This has my entire approval" (*Alternative 3:* see Document 17).

There was one problem. Wilson lacked any legal authority to grant financial support to an unrecognized political group. Lansing's thought was to arrange for the money to be loaned to the British and French, who could be trusted to handle the transfer discreetly. That solution raised another difficulty: America would become involved in the schemes of Allied policy makers, but not be able to exercise control over them. It was the same issue as that posed by Japanese intervention in Siberia. Apparently Wilson and Lansing decided it was a lesser risk than the danger of disclosure and embarrassment.

As it turned out, no American money was needed. Historians agree, however, that a major decision of principle had occurred, and an important precedent set for later decisions concerning intervention. The decision of principle involved was a decision against alternative 1: recognition of the Soviet government. What historians disagree about is the motive behind the decision. To some students of American policy, this early decision represents a clear-cut determination to drive the Bolsheviks from power by whatever means available. Others argue that the primary concern was to sustain the Eastern Front—there would have been no intervention then or later had there been no war. In this context it might be noted that Wilson was not only setting a precedent for later actions in Russia, but following precedents already established in dealing with the Mexican Revolution.

From the time of Huerta's disappearance from the Mexican scene the president had maintained agents at the headquarters of each of the revolutionary leaders—even after Carranza had established a government in Mexico City. Lansing explained candidly that the primary reason for encouraging one of these leaders, Villa, was to keep open the question of diplomatic recognition:

> The reason for furnishing Villa with an opportunity to obtain funds is this: We do not wish the Carranza faction to be the only one to deal with in Mexico. Carranza seems so impossible that an appearance at least, of opposition to him will give us an opportunity to invite a compromise of factions. I think, therefore, it is politic, for the time, to allow Villa to obtain sufficient financial resources to allow his faction to remain in arms until a compromise can be effected.[3]

The disagreement among scholars is not insurmountable, moreover, if it is agreed that Wilson had ruled out diplomatic recognition of the Soviets as an alternative. Nonrecognition was a necessary step toward reaching the second level of Wilson's response to the Bolshevik revolution.

Wilson's War Aims Endangered: The Road to Brest-Litovsk

Various observers and friends had warned the president that Lenin posed the most serious threat to the achievement of American war aims. Indirectly, it was argued in American circles, the Allies were to blame because their refusal to reconsider "their" war aims had been responsible for Kerensky's debacle and accounted for much of the support the Bolsheviks received from non-Marxist sources. If that sympathy was not counteracted promptly and effectively, one of two things (both bad) would be likely to happen: the world liberal movement would split up over Bolshevism, weakening itself fatally and/or the reactionaries would use bolshevism to discredit Wilsonian goals.

At this critical juncture Wilson delivered the first of two speeches aimed at regaining the initiative. On December 4, 1917, he asked Congress to declare war on Austria, using the occasion to state that if Allied war aims had been made plain at the outset of the war (meaning of course *his* and not those of the Allies), and had the Russian people believed in them, the sad reverses which had taken place since Kerensky's demise might never have occurred. But, he went on, the Russian people had been duped by the very same falsehoods that had misled the German people. Behind these lies lurked a dark conspiracy against all peoples who wanted a world made safe for democracy.

Wilson hoped to accomplish several things with this speech. First, he reaffirmed that the war was a just war; next, he implied that the United States had taken charge of Allied war aims; and finally, he made effective use of the "agent" theory to account for the sad reverses of the Russian

Revolution. If "liberal" elements did indeed exist in Russia, Wilson's words offered them a purified set of goals worth fighting for, but the agent theory had to be handled with care. To the CPI's Edgar Sisson, "The President's words read . . . like orders from home."[4] Sisson may have interpreted his "orders" to mean that he should produce proof of the agent thesis, which he promptly set out to do, thereby contributing to Wilson's dilemma, though certainly the president was predisposed toward that blind alley anyway.

Better known was the January 8, 1918, Fourteen Points speech, in which the president referred to the "voice of the Russian people." Without mentioning Lenin, Wilson lauded the "Russian representatives" for their insistence on open negotiations at Brest-Litovsk, the scene of the peace discussions with Germany. Using Russian attitudes and actions, Wilson had performed a real feat, wiping the slate clean of the secret treaties and seizing the initiative for his new diplomacy (*Alternative 3:* see Document 18).

Several of the Fourteen Points referred to Russia and Russian conditions, but the president had taken the initiative from Trotsky by going beyond the release of secret treaties, as the Bolsheviks had done, to demanding: "Open Covenants of peace, openly arrived at, after which there shall be no private international understandings of any kind, but diplomacy shall proceed always frankly and in the public view." Wilson did not deny what Lenin insisted the secret treaties proved; he did not sidestep the imperialism of all parties involved in the present war; nor did he deny that the political and economic roots of war were imperialism and the alliance system. What he promised was a fundamental change in the relations of nation to nation.

The Fourteen Points speech successfully established Wilson as the spokesman for world liberalism, but it did not exempt him from renewed pressures from Allied leaders to do something about Russia. In fact the Allies were most upset about the very issue Wilson had singled out to praise the Bolsheviks: Their conduct of "open" peace negotiations with the Central Powers at Brest-Litvosk. To the Allies it made very little idfference whether Lenin's representatives appealed to American sensibilities as latter-day Ben Franklins in coonskin headgear negotiating with the bigwigs of old world diplomacy or not. Wilson could think what he liked about the virtues of "open convenants of peace, openly arrived at" but the Bolsheviks had endangered Anglo-French interests by sitting down to talk with the enemy. And they lost no opportunity to tell Wilson so.

Russian overtures for an armistice and peace treaty had begun almost as soon as the Bolsheviks took power. Trotsky had announced to the world his government's intentions, concluding with a stern warning: "If the allied nations do not send their representatives, we shall conduct negotiations alone with the Germans. We want a general peace, but if the bourgeois in the allied countries force us to conclude a separate peace the entire responsibility will be theirs."[5]

Wilson's Fourteen Points speech was not a sufficient answer, argued the Allies. The president must do something to prevent Lenin from carrying out this threat. But Wilson had declared in that speech that Russia was to be the acid test of the good will of her sister nations in the months to come. Alright, said the Allies in so many words, then let Wilson help them discipline and control her behavior. Wilson had never meant to approve of a separate Russo-German peace treaty, but he was on the spot. He had used, or tried to use, Russia's claims that it was conducting open negotiations with the Germans to launch his own program of open diplomacy, and to top Trotsky's release of the secret treaties. The distinction, perfectly clear to him (and necessary to his conduct of American foreign relations) was not always clear to others.

In this ambiguous situation there seemed to a few Allied and American representatives one way out that would serve everyone's basic interests. These men began from the premise that Trotsky's public declarations were not his last words on the subject of peace with Germany, especially if Berlin's negotiators should demand an outrageous price for peace. The weakness of their position was that for Wilson to go along with their efforts to influence the Bolshevik leaders, he would have to reconsider his decision not to have direct dealings with Lenin. He could, consistent with his chosen policy of "watchful waiting," wait to see what developed of these informal contacts, and then decide.

Out on a Limb with Raymond Robins

Those who argued for a reassessment of the Russian situation conceded that it might not be possible to sustain the fighting on the Eastern Front, but that even so it was well worth the effort to try to influence the Bolshevik position in the peace negotiations. To do this would mean, in all likelihood, not only informal contacts but eventually diplomatic recognition and economic aid. The first such policy recommendation came from General William V. Judson, head of the American military mission in Russia. Judson's encounters with Trotsky had convinced him there was something to be gained for American interests from such an approach and, more important, that to ignore Lenin's government was to play Germany's game. Press reports of the general's activities were not well received in Washington. Disavowed by Ambassador Francis, Judson was recalled by the War Department. Under-lining its attitude on these matters, the State Department then cabled specific instructions that American representatives were to withhold all direct communication with the Bolshevik government.

A more serious and long-lasting effort to change the direction of Bolshevik and American policies to permit parallel action, if not cooperation, vis-a-vis Germany originated with Colonel Raymond Robins. Robins's military title was honorific and only temporary. It was given to him for protocol purposes when he was attached to the American Red Cross mission in Russia. Unlike Judson, who was subject to close War Department supervision, Robins, a midwestern Progressive, had access to powerful friends in political circles. Unlike Judson, Robins's meetings with Trotsky did not constitute any hint of recognition since the Red Cross did not "represent" the United States government. In short, he could be a very useful go-between for everyone concerned.

For more than two months Robins moved back and forth between Francis and Trotsky, seizing upon the slightest sign that either side was ready to change course. Trotsky, as Robins and others had predicted, *was* disturbed by German demands at Brest-Litvosk. He seemed to be groping for some formula to explain the situation to ideologues on the party's central committee. He had come up with the "no war, no peace" slogan, which he no doubt hoped would stave off a German offensive if the talks finally broke down. Still, he had doubts; and in this state of mind he maintained contacts with Allied representatives, thus giving Robins his opening. Russo-German negotiations did breakdown, and on February 18, 1918, German military operations recommenced. Trotsky then appeared before his colleagues on the central committee, and asked them to forego doctrinal purity by accepting aid from the capitalist governments. There was no question of obligations, explained Trotsky, only aid to arm and equip the Red army.

This sort of proposal and debate takes place at some stage in nearly every revolutionary situation, and within each individual revolutionary conscience. The commissar for Foreign Affairs was asking them to abandon "internationalism," to betray the working class of the world. Trotsky could have added that the working class of the belligerent countries had shown little disposition to come to Russia's aid thus far, but his motion was carried anyway by a narrow margin, six votes to five. Lenin was not present at the meeting, but had asked that his vote be recorded along with an explanation: "I request you to add my vote in favour of taking potatoes and ammunition from the Anglo-French imperialist robbers."[6] He cited as precedent for his action the decision of American revolutionary leaders to accept aid from France and Spain in their struggle against George III of England.

Yet within twenty-four hours the central committee reversed itself by voting to accept a German ultimatum, and the Treaty of Brest-Litovsk was signed. Robins and other Allied agents who believed as he did, still refused to give up—the treaty had not yet been ratified. On March 2, 1918, the Soviets heard rumors that Japan was about to intervene at Vladivostok. Almost in a state of panic, Lenin and Trotsky despatched a friendly French diplomat to the American ambassador with a message begging Francis to intercede with his government to prevent a Japanese landing. They also offered a new inducement, the possibility of Allied cooperation in organizing a Russian army, based on equalitarian principles, for service against Germany.

Three days later Trotsky asked Robins if he wanted to prevent the treaty from being ratified. If the Red Cross colonel could get a definite promise of aid from his government, it could be done. Robins reacted cautiously, What about Lenin, he asked? He was running the show, wasn't he, and he favored accepting the treaty. Trotsky replied that Robins was mistaken, and that Lenin himself would agree in writing to fight the Germans if he could be sure of Allied economic and military support. Robins left Trotsky's office to report this development, and to give the Russians time to produce such a document. When he returned a few hours later, he received a formal message for transmission. A careful reading of the wording of the Russian statement reveals that it was not quite so clear-cut as Robins later contended (see Document 19); nevertheless, even with the hedges Trotsky included, the Bolsheviks had made a serious offer—at least worthy of investigation.

This does not mean that either Trotsky or Lenin (the more skeptical) ever saw American aid as an alternative to ratification. It may well have been a ploy to delay or deter the feared Japanese landing in Siberia. Trotsky's written proposal included a query concerning American willingness to prevent such a landing. Robins later told the story that on the night the Congress of Soviets met to discuss the treaty, Lenin approached him to ask if he had heard anything from his government. When he received a negative reply, Lenin said that he would speak for the treaty—and it would be ratified. Those who doubt the significance of this episode point out that Lenin had never really looked favorably upon Allied and American aid as a logical policy for Russia, and that (if the scene actually took place) the Bolshevik leader was merely interested in proving a point to Robins: that his government would never consider aid to the Soviets. Everyone agrees Lenin did prove his point.

Be that as it may, the suggestion that Lenin had to persuade the Soviet Congress to accept the harsh terms of the treaty poses something of a problem for those who insist that the Bolsheviks would have remained inflexible regardless of what Wilson did or did not do about the Trotsky inquiry. What if the answer had been yes? Lenin could not very well have concealed that from the congress, and as had already become evident, the central committee was itself divided over the issue. Lenin did need to know, therefore, if there had been any response from Washington, so that he could at least take it into account in his speech. Second, Robins was not alone in his belief that in March, 1918, the Bolshevik leadership was ready to consider seriously a working relationship with America and the Allies. The same fear of Japan which had led Trotsky to include a reference to the Far Eastern question in his proposal, if no other reason, was a possible stimulus to normalization of relations with America and the other Allies.

Perhaps Robins, and his British counterpart, R. Bruce Lockhart, were simply under Lenin's spell. That would explain why they continued to cling to the slightest hope for reasonable relations with unreasonable men who had denounced their governments and all their works. But Lenin seemed equally blunt when he told Lockhart that the Bolsheviks could afford to compromise temporarily with capital. Ratification of the Treaty of Brest-Litvosk did not mean that Russia would become a granary for the Central Powers. Passive resistance, Lenin told Lockhart, was a more potent weapon than an army that cannot fight. When Lockhart and Robins pondered Lenin's words, they concluded that their governments were missing an important opportunity.

They may well have been mistaken. We simply do not know what effect a solid offer of American aid would have made in any of these contingencies, before or after ratification of the treaty, because such an offer was never made. At the moment when the central committee of the Bolshevik party had first considered accepting Allied support, in mid-February, 1918, the French sounded American opinion on the idea. Lansing took the proposal to the president for a decision. On the message he noted in pencil: "This is out of the question. Submitted to Pres't who says the same thing." [7]

At the urging of advisers in the United States, Wilson did make an appeal to the Congress of Soviets against ratification. The message of sympathy for the plight of the Russian people, noted Colonel House, was "one of the most cleverly worded, three sentenced messages extant." It explained that the United States was not in a position to aid Russia at the moment, and was addressed not to the Congress, but to the "people of Russia through the Soviet Congress," (see Document 20). It was hardly the sort of message one would send to encourage a nation's faith in its leaders; instead there was a clear suggestion that the revolutionary government was not responsive to the will of the people and had become the instrument of some foreign power seeking to enslave them.

From Wilson's point of view the terms of the Brest-Litovsk Treaty itself made the case. One provision—the most damning against the Bolsheviks— required Russia to recognize a separate German treaty with the Ukraine, which had proclaimed its independence. As a direct result of Bolshevik rule, it was now argued, the old Russian Empire was being picked apart: could things have been any worse whether or not the Communists were German agents? Historian-diplomat George Frost Kennan points out that even more than the specific provisions concerning the Ukraine and other areas, the real impact of the Brest-Litovsk Treaty was the general feeling it produced in Washington: ". . . the settlement represented a bilateral arrangement, anticipating the general peace conference to which he [Wilson] aspired. Worst of all, by sanctioning a species of German intervention into Russian affairs, the settlement provided precedent and further incentive for a similar Japanese incursion in the Russian Far East: a prospect embarrassing and displeasing to American statemanship. A separate Russian-German treaty thus actually prejudiced the prospects for a general Wilsonian peace both in Asia and in Europe."

A Mandate For Intervention?

To the Allies the Brest-Litvosk Treaty provided a mandate for intervention. "Up to the moment when the Bolshevik Government decided to accept the peace terms, I was opposed to Japanese intervention," British Foreign Secretary Arthur J. Balfour cabled Colonel House on March 6, 1918, "as I hoped Bolshevik resistance to German aggression might continue. When the Bolsheviki surrendered unconditionally, it became of the utmost importance to prevent the rich supplies in Siberia from falling into German hands, and the only method by which this could be secured was by Japanese intervention on a considerable scale." [8] Balfour's explanation was a bit too pat. As early as December 14, 1917, the British had put forward a suggestion for a possible Japanese intervention to secure the eastern terminus of the Trans-Siberian Railroad. At that time Lansing had spoken directly to the Japanese ambassador, expressing strong disapproval for any such scheme.

Nevertheless, by January, 1918, Japan had four ships standing off Vladivostok in readiness to undertake an Allied mandate. Tokyo thus practiced its own "watchful waiting" policy, not unlike Wilson's orders to the American fleet in the Gulf of Mexico four years earlier. The president had finally given the command to occupy Vera Cruz, but he did not want the Japanese to exercise a similar mandate on his behalf—or anyone else's—for the occupation of Vladivostok. His first response was to send the *U.S.S. Brooklyn* to Vladivostok to remind everyone concerned that the United States expected to be consulted in matters of such high policy. Repeated efforts to convince Wilson to join in asking the Japanese to accept this "responsibility" on behalf of all the powers at war with Germany got nowhere. The president always responded that a Japanese "invasion" would produce only support for the Bolsheviks.

Japanese war aims were a frequent subject in Washington conversations. Had not the Japanese used the war to advance their special position in China? What further plans did they now have for Siberia? What hopes did they *not* entertain? As the British saw it, the question of Japanese penetration had to be faced sooner or later: better, then, that Tokyo should act with the blessing (and under the control) of the Allies than unilaterally. Secretary Lansing became convinced by these arguments, writing to Wilson that since "Japan intends to go into Siberia anyway" it would be best to have it done under Allied auspices with formal pledges from Tokyo of Japanese "disinterestedness" and willingness to carry on military activities up to the Ural mountains. To be effective against the Germans, a Japanese intervention would have to go at least that far. Thus, ironically, a pledge of disinterestedness could only be fulfilled by a Japanese military advance "to the confines of Asia." Lansing argued that Wilson did not have to encourage the Japanese, only stipulate that the United States would not protest the action.

Wilson and Lansing considered the Siberian problem on the morning of March 1, 1918. When they finished the discussion, the president sat down to type a draft for the Allied ambassadors *(Alternative 2:* see Document 21). It stated that the United States would not object if the Allies wanted to request Japanese intervention, so long as everyone understood that a final settlement of the Siberian issue must await the peace conference. Hedged as it was, this formula still seemed dangerous to some, especially as it appeared to disregard Bolshevik appeals for American assurances against Japanese military action. Were the Communists to be allowed to pass themselves off as the only real Russian nationalists?

Boris Bakhmeteff, ambassador of the still-recognized Provisional Government, hurried to New York to warn Colonel House of the consequences of such policy. Taking no chances, he sent another embassy official to the State Department to argue that the "sole intervention" of Japan would produce an unmitigated disaster *(Alternative 2:* see Document 22). A Far Eastern intervention could succeed only if the United States, Great Britain and France also sent troops, thereby blunting the fear of Japanese aggression.

Meanwhile, Wilson had been having second thoughts of his own, and when Colonel House's letter arrived urging reconsideration, the president put a new sheet in his typewriter. This time the note to the Allied ambassadors stated that no matter what assurances the Japanese offered, intervention would play into the hands of "the enemies of the Russian revolution" (see Document 23). By Wilson's definition, of course, the Bolsheviks were enemies of the Russian revolution.

The president was still searching for an effective means of opposing the Bolsheviks. His own conclusion, bolstered by advice from military experts and other observers, was that the German threat to Siberia was an Allied chimera; conversely, the prospects of a serious attack against German forces through Siberia appeared to him almost equally unrealistic. One diplomat whom Wilson did trust was his ambassador to China, Paul S. Reinsch, who kept him posted on the situation as it appeared from Peking (see Document 24). There was information from Reinsch, and from other observers, that the democratic spirit Wilson knew must be present somewhere in the vast Russian heartland had sprung up in Siberia itself.

On April 18, 1918, Wilson wrote his secretary of state that he desired a memorandum containing all that was known about the several nuclei of self-governing authority that seemed to be springing up in Siberia. It would afford him a great deal of satisfaction to get behind the most nearly representative if it could draw support from Siberia. In the meantime, Wilson alerted British officials that it was necessary to be ready to move when the right time came. When that moment arrived, America would enter Siberia not as a disguised conqueror or bogus mandatory, but to support the principle of self-government. American intervention would be concerned with bringing essential support to men determined to rescue themselves from the past as well as from the Bolsheviks. The great beauty of this plan was that it would contain the Japanese forward movement on the Asian mainland (the last military threat to a Wilsonian peace once Germany was defeated), and finally absorb it into American policy. Wilson moved carefully in implementing (and protecting) his chosen alternative because it represented a delicate balance between conflicting pressures and antagonistic ideologies.

Notes

1. Quoted by E.H. Carr, *The Bolshevik Revolution, 1917-1923* 3 vols. (London: MacMillan & Co. 1952-54), III, 16.

2. *Ibid.*

3. Robert Lansing to Woodrow Wilson, August 9, 1915, Papers of Woodrow Wilson, Library of Congress, Washington, D.C.

4. Edgar Sisson, *One Hundred Red Days: A Personal Chronicle of the Bolshevik Revolution* (New Haven: Yale University Press, 1931), p. 112.

5. Wireless Appeal By the Council of People's Commissars to the Peoples of the Belligerent Countries to Join in the Negotiations for an Armistice, November 28, 1917, in Jane Degras, ed., *Soviet Documents on Foreign Policy, 1917-1924* (New York: Oxford Univ. Press, 1951), pp. 11-12.

6. Carr, *The Bolshevik Revolution,* III, 46.

7. Pencilled notation by Lansing, February 19, 1918, *Papers of the Department of State,* Decimal File 861.00/1125, National Archives, Washington, D.C.

8. Quoted in, Charles Seymour, ed., *The Intimate Papers of Colonel House,* 4 vols. (Boston: Houghton-Mifflin, 1926-28), III, 397-98.

5

The Justification for Intervention

Balfour had expressed the opinion that the Treaty of Brest- Litovsk was ample justification for an intervention policy based on simple military necessity; Wilson had demanded more. How deeply did he look into the policy he was about to undertake? Even though he agonized about Russia for days at a time, there is room to speculate. But this much seems clear: he had convinced himself that his course was the only disinterested approach to Russian affairs, whether compared to the policy of the Germans, the Japanese, or even the Allied high command in Europe. With the March revolution, Russia had become part of the solution to Wilson's foreign policy problems in dealing with reactionary nations. Now Russia was at the center of those problems. Beyond this, he believed the Bolsheviks must fail—and that they must not be allowed to take the rest of his postwar plans down with them. Other developments contributed to a rationale for intervention which seemingly led the president to depart from his own principle of national self-determination. Viewed from another perspective, however, Wilson was consistent: the Bolsheviks professed an international solidarity among the workingclasses of the world. It was they who denied the validity of national self-determination—for Russia or for anyone else—except to protect themselves until they were strong enough to take the offensive against world capitalism. Since the Bolsheviks had deprived Russia or self-determination, continued this line of reasoning, it would have to be imposed from without. Here was paradox on the grand scale.

Nearly every pronouncement from the Smolny Institute, where Lenin had established himself, gave further proof of Bolshevik hostility to all capitalist nations. But it was Lenin's contempt for the Constituent Assembly which allowed Wilson to claim that the Communists had denied Russia self-determination. In the only free elections ever held in Soviet Russia, on November 25, 1917, the Bolsheviks secured less than a third of the seats in the Constituent Assembly. Having defeated the Provisional Government in the streets of Petrograd, were they now to be defeated by its ghost? The Provisional Government had been responsible for scheduling these elections for a Constituent Assembly, which, it had been decided, would undertake the task of drafting a constitution for a permanent national government.

Before they seized power the Bolsheviks had cast themselves as the saviors of the Constituent Assembly against those who were determined to destroy it. But now Lenin had a different view. The Bolsheviks had demonstrated great strength in the cities, but not enough to overcome the moderates, who enjoyed peasant support, and who claimed a majority of the seats. There was little doubt in Lenin's mind that the assembly would try to turn back the clock in Russia. When it met he ordered, and joined in, harassment tactics. The moderates refused to be intimidated and kept the meeting going until after four o'clock in the morning of January 19, 1918, passing resolution after resolution. Exasperated by this defiance, the Bolsheviks issued a decree dissolving the assembly, to take effect at ten o'clock that same day.

By so doing, However, Lenin had severely weakened Bolshevik claims to legitimacy as the *de jure* government of Russia, the test Wilson had applied to Huerta's Mexico and which the dictator had failed in 1913. On this question, at least, British and American officials saw eye to eye. At the end of January, Colonel House forwarded to the president a letter from a British policy maker which put the case as Wilson himself might have stated it. The forced dissolution of the Constituent Assembly, wrote House's informant, made the Bolshevik claim no better than that of the autonomous body in South East Russia.

Wilson's continuing interest in the "Sisson" papers indicates his need for constant reassurance at every step as he moved from "watchful waiting" toward positive intervention. In March, 1918, the president personally ordered the Committee on Public Information representative to proceed directly to Washington with the material he had purchased from anti-Bolshevik sources. Secretary Lansing's own investigation of these documents persuaded him that it would be a mistake to publish them as United States government certified. Nevertheless, Wilson ordered it done in September, 1918.

By that time American troops were already on their way to Siberia; and Wilson needed all the support he could muster to fend off critics. The troop decision was reached in July, but the immediate origins of the decision went back to the end of May when Washington learned of the plight of the Czechoslovakian troops who were then attempting to make their way east along the Trans-Siberian Railroad to Vladivostok. They had been promised safe passage out of Russia so long as they kept to themselves. The Czechs had accepted these terms as the only way they could find transportation to a port from which they could then reach the Western Front. Incidents occurred—perhaps stimulated by Allied military advisers accompanying the Czechs—and Trotsky demanded that they be disarmed. This led to a series of armed clashes, and soon the Czechs controlled long stretches of the Trans-Siberian line.

Ambassador Reinsch out in China thought he saw a real possibility that the Czechs could play an even more heroic role. Hence he advised Washington that it would be unwise to remove the Czechs from Siberia. With only minimum support from outside they could control all Siberia, and hold it against the Germans. Sympahtetic to the Russian population, they were also eager to aid the Allied cause. Their removal would further discourage loyal Russia. Indeed, were they not already in Siberia, it would have been worthwhile to bring them there.

Wilson was struck by the idea. "There seems to me to emerge from this suggestion," he noted to Lansing, "the shadow of a plan that might be worked, with Japanese and other assistance. These people are the cousins of the Russians."[1]

Having gone to war on the Allied side in 1917, how much freedom of action did Wilson actually have in resisting their demands for intervention? He might, and did, doubt that their motives for the intervention were what they said they were. Sir Edward Grey had told Colonel House at the time of sinking of the *Lusitania* (1915) that if President Wilson expected to have a significant voice in the peace settlement he would have to take a stand on submarine warfare. That factor was surely present in Wilson s mind as he pondered what was best for him to do in regard to Russia. He could not very well save Siberia for the Russians if a hostile Allied combine, from which he had excluded himself, had different ideas. He could stand out against the Allies when the time came if he had done his share in bearing the burden when the going was tough. It was not a happy prospect, but Wilson must have wondered if it was his best chance after all.

The Great Siberian Adventure

The decision to send troops to Siberia was reached at a White House conference on July 6, 1918. Japan and America would each send seven thousand troops, whose primary mission would be to guard the line of communication of the Czecho-Slovaks. It was also decided to issue a public statement that the sending of these contingents constituted no purpose to interfere with internal affairs of Russia or with the political or territorial soverignty of Russia. An American *aide-memoire* to the Allied ambassadors dated July 17 described the mission of the troops as being "to steady any efforts at self-government or self-defense in which the Russians themselves may be willing to accept assistance" (see Document 25). The Czechs had taken up arms, it will be remembered, to secure a route *out* of Russia. Wilson's proposal, following Reinsch's line of reasoning, depended upon their staying *in* Russia. The final paragraph of the July 17 *aide-memoire*, moreover, set forth the president's intention to send an economic mission to Siberia.

General Tasker H. Bliss, the American representative on the Supreme War Council, thought he knew exactly what result was expected: "If the Japanese and the other Allies strengthen the Czecho-Slovaks, I cannot see that it can have any other object than to overturn the present so-called Government in Russia." Later commentators have pointed out that the size of the intervention force Wilson approved ruled out even the remotest possibility that the Siberian expedition could be employed to overthrow the Soviet government. Certainly the Allies were disappointed by Wilson's limitations on the size of the force. British Prime Minister David Lloyd George complained that the president seemed to have misunderstood the scale of effort necessary to achieve any result. Lloyd George had in mind the reopening of the Eastern Front. But it was probably the other way around: the Allied leaders had misunderstood. The president had never imagined a march on Berlin or Petrograd. His premise was that there *were* elements in Russia, particularly in

Siberia which could be strengthened into positive forces which could stand on their own against the spread of Bolshevism. Lenin understood the situation better than the Allies (see Document 26).

Historians who generally take the position that the American phase of the intervention was not motivated primarily by anti-Bolshevik feelings and determinations nevertheless conclude that the Siberian venture was launched with something more in mind than the simple rescue of the Czech soldiers. Thus Kennan again:

> But was it his [Wilson's] intention that the Czechs should serve as a spearhead for action against the Bolsheviki?
> The most likely answer to this question is that both Lansing and the President secretly hoped that the arrival of American and Japanese forces would elicit so powerful and friendly a reaction among the population that a pro-Allied political authority would be instituted throughout Siberia by spontaneous, democratic action. This might, in turn, lead to the prevalence of a new pro-Allied spirit in Russia proper, which in turn would either come to permeate the policies of the Bolsheviki or cause them to yield to other political forces more responsive to the political will.[2]

A massive influx of Allied troops, especially Japanese forces, would only defeat Wilson's purpose. Once the armistice with Germany was signed in November, 1918, the president ordered Secretary Lansing to make representations against the further expansion of Japanese occupation forces which had grown from seven thousand to more than seventy thousand. In addition, the United States insisted that the key Siberian railways be put under an inter-Allied commission headed by John F. Stevens. Irrespective of what America's future policy toward Russia might be, Lansing explained to congressional critics, "it is essential that we maintain the policy of the open door with reference to the Siberian and particularly the Chinese Eastern Railway" (see Document 27).

By locating the intervention squarely within the framework of America's traditional open door policy in the Far East, Wilson no doubt hoped to blunt criticism of the decision to maintain American troops in Siberia. The American commander in Siberia, General William S. Graves, was already fed up, and wrote to his superiors that "this crowd [the anti-Bolshevik government] could not remain in power 24 hours in eastern Siberia after allied troops are removed" (see Document 28). His original hopes already dimming, Wilson clung tenaciously to China policy principles (or dogma) in evaluating the Russian situation. Just as the United States had taken on responsibility for the territorial and political integrity of China, Wilson now asserted that Washington had an equal obligation to defend Russia against supposed plots—even if that entailed involvement in the civil war. The justification was becoming more and more complicated. "The primary concern of American military forces," a historian wrote about the American military presence in Siberia, "now became the restoration and protection of the railways instead of the rescue of the Czechs. The latter were now participating in the execution of the railway plan. In effect, the improvement of the transportation system served to aid the anti-Bolshevik cause. Thus, despite its denials, the United States became an active participant in the Russian Civil War."[3]

Bolshevism and Peacemaking

Under the terms of the November, 1918 armistice with the Central Powers, Germany was, in effect, charged with the responsibility of containing the spread of Bolshevism in Eastern Europe until a more permanent solution could be devised. Article 12, for example, stipulated that German evacuation of occupied eastern territories would be held up until "the Allies think the moment suitable, having regard to the internal situation of these territories." In return, Wilson personally accepted responsibility for taking up with the Allies the "supplying of foodstuffs to Germany," provided he could "be assured that public order is being and will continue to be maintained in Germany...." The focus of Allied and American diplomacy shifted to Europe with the armistice, and to the danger of Bolshevism spreading west into the heart of Central Europe. Wilson's insistence that America could not deal with the kaiser's government had been a powerful stimulus to the revolution which brought into being a German Provisional Government. Was the Russian pattern about to be repeated? Secretary Lansing, for one, was afraid it might be. "How much encouragement should we give to radicalism in Germany," he wrote Elihu Root, "in the effort to crush out Prussianism? We cannot dismiss these questions with an assertion of disbelief that Bolshevism cannot become a factor among an enlightened people, because the doctrine of the 'social revolution' is gaining adherents in every land. This we know."[4]

The answer Lansing sought emerged from the Versailles Conference. Rival congresses met in Europe at the beginning of 1919. In Paris the victors assembled to write a peace treaty; in Moscow delegates from Communist parties and socialist movements around the world gathered to write a "constitution" for the Communist International. At its final session, the Moscow congress addressed an appeal "to the Workers of All Countries," calling upon them to use all means available "including, if necessary, revolutionary means" to force an end to the intervention, withdrawal of foreign armies from Russia, and diplomatic recognition of the Soviet regime. Despite its dominance by Russian figures (thirty-five out of fifty delegates), the new Communist International appeared to exert a powerful influence over labor forces in the West and revolutionary nationalists in the East.

"Hands-off Russia" demonstrations and rallies in Great Britain, the proclamation of a German Soviet Republic in Munich, and the rise of Bela Kun's Communist government in Budapest, seemed proof of a revolutionary "conspiracy" emanating from Petrograd. Soviet writers almost gleefully predicted that the authors of the Versailles Treaty had concocted a powerful revolutionary potion. Even the sober Lenin, who had been disappointed that more than a year had gone by without major new outbreaks, announced that the Versailles treaty would stimulate an immense revolutionary movement in Germany. Colonel House recorded his private apprehensions that the

Bolsheviks might just be right: "Bolshevism is gaining ground everywhere. Hungary has just succumbed. We are sitting upon an open powder magazine and some day a spark may ignite it."[5]

At the first meeting of the council of Ten at Versailles on January 12, 1919, the French confronted Wilson with a proposal to send Allied troops into Poland to help organize anti-Bolshevik forces there. Faced with the stark reality of a military alternative, the president stalled for time. Such a scheme, he said, "formed part of the much larger question of checking the advance of Bolshevism westward." He had great doubts "as to whether this advance could be checked by arms at all." Joining Wilson was Lloyd George, who had also developed serious doubts about the military alternative. On January 16, the British prime minister outlined three possible ways of dealing with the Bolsheviks, concluding that the best was to summon representatives of all factions "to appear before those present, somewhat in the way that the Roman Empire summoned chiefs of outlying tributary states to render an account of their actions."

"On the other hand," he ended, "if a military enterprise were started against the Bolsheviki, that would make England Bolshevist, and there would be a Soviet in London." Wilson picked up on the prime minister's theme, adding that the "whole world" had been disturbed by the labor-capital question before Lenin came into power. "Seeds need soil, and the Bolsheviki seeds found the soil already prepared for them" (see Document 29). The president took to the idea of a conference of all the warring factions at once. Lloyd George's plan envisioned a meeting on Prinkipo Island in the Sea of Marmara—a remote place selected because the Soviet delegates would not have to travel through any third country—between representatives of the rival governments in Russia and emissaries of the Great Powers.

In advancing his plan, the prime minister seemed to be moving in the direction of diplomatic dealings with the Bolsheviks, despite his analogy of the Roman Empire and tributary states. Wilson, however, stressed that the Prinkipo Conference would undercut the moral influence of the Bolsheviks by demonstrating that the Allies had no intention of restoring the old regime in Russia. By encouraging the representatives of these organized groups in Russia to "put all their cards on the table, and see if they could not come to an understanding," the result would be to "bring about more reaction against the cause of the Bolsheviki than anything else the Allies could do."

The Prinkipo scheme never came off. Encouraged by the French, who assured them that they need not risk anything on such a fanciful endeavor, the various "white" (anti-Bolshevik) factions declined. Left with only a favorable response from Lenin's government, the embarrassed Allies declared that the primary conditions for the meeting had not been satisfied. In conservative eyes, however, the thought of dealing with the Bolsheviks even on that level was enough to give both Lloyd George and Wilson black marks. The president's initial attraction to the idea may have had to do with the pattern of his diplomacy in the Mexican Revolution. He had subsidized Carranza's rivals in the vain hope that at some point such a conference would be held in Mexico, and from it would emerge a "provisional" government committed to his ideal of free elections and liberal democracy. However that may be, Wilson continued to subsidize the Provisional Government's embassy in Washington out of secret funds appropriated by Congress during the war, apparently in the hope that when the true Russian spirit revived it would be ready to resume its natural functions.

In the meantime, some of the president's advisers thought it might be worthwhile to test hints that propaganda against the capitalist powers would come to an end when the victors made their peace with Russia. Maxim Litvinov, an important Bolshevik diplomat, had told a minor American official that in certain western countries conditions were not favorable for a revolution. Litvinov had added that Russia was anxious to resume economic relations with the West, a point also made in the Bolshevik response to the Prinkipo invitation. Indeed, on that occasion, the Soviet foreign commissar had gone so far as to say that his government did not refuse to recognize its financial obligations to Allied creditors, and that it was willing to grant economic concessions to nationals of the Allied powers, so long as they were operated in a way that would not conflict with the economic and social order of Soviet Russia.

Lenin's statement could be considered as an invitation to the Allies either to underwrite the success of the communist order with capitalist money or to confess that the desire for special concessions was the mainspring of capitalist foreign policy. Obviously Wilson could not open relations with Lenin on either basis, but it might be possible to see what the leader of the world's first Communist nation had on his mind about a possible truce in what could already be called a "Cold War" between East and West. In the president's absence, Secretary Lansing and Colonel House took it upon themselves to send a junior member of the American Peace Mission, William C. Bullitt, to explore possibilities of a *modus vivendi* with Lenin. Bullitt came back from Moscow with a document signed by Lenin embodying some of what Litvinov had promised verbally in earlier meetings. One point in the proposed agreement would have opened up the "Allied and Associated countries as well as . . . all countries which have been formed on the territory of the former Russian Empire and Finland" to citizens of the Soviet Republics of Russia, in exchange for a like privilege for nationals of the Allied and Associated countries in Russia. In both cases the right of travel and sojourn was to be conditioned on assurances of noninterference in the domestic politics of the host country. But as Lenin confided to Lincoln Steffens, an American journalist who had accompanied Bullitt to Moscow, "A propagandist . . . is a propagandist. . . . If our borders are opened our propagandists will go to Europe and propagand, just as yours will come here and propagand. We can agree not to send them to you, and we can agree that if they do go, they shall be subject to your laws, but we—nobody can make a propagandist stop propaganding."[6]

That statement, candid as it was, explains why Bullitt's efforts went to nought. No assurances from Lenin, even if he had stated that exact opposite of what he did say to Steffens, could have satisfied Wilson that by dealing with the Russian leader he was not opening the West to Communist "propaganda." Wilson did not even receive Bullitt upon his return. Thinking he had been authorized to negotiate such a truce, Bullitt was deeply angered. Conditions had changed since House and Lansing first proposed the mission. Now there was a Bolshevik government in Hungary under the leadership of Bela Kun posing a distinct threat to Central Europe and Germany. It was a difficult time for anyone who advocated even limited dealings with the Soviets.

Once again the French proposed a military alternative for dealing with Bela Kun. Wilson responded during a meeting of the Big Four on March 25, 1919, that his policy was to leave Russia to the Bolsheviks: "Let the Russians stew in their own juice until circumstances have made them wiser, and let us confine our efforts to keeping Bolshevism out of the rest of Europe." The next day he asked Herbert Hoover, the former head of American relief operations in Europe, for his thoughts on the Russian problem. Since coming to Versailles Hoover had been occupied trying to convince the Allies of the folly of continuing an economic blockade against the defeated nations. His intense dislike of the Bolsheviks did not blind him to the essential problem facing Europe: the resumption of production and distribution. One did better to feed potential revolutionaries, he argued, than to fight starving men. If the United States took part in a military intervention against Bela Kun, it would mean lending support to the most reactionary forces on the Continent (*Alternative 2:* see Document 30).

Hoover's counterproposal had one very big advantage over the Lenin-Bullitt agreement: no diplomatic dealings were involved. With Wilson's support, Hoover proposed to the Big Four nations that a declaration be issued informing the people of Hungary that the tasks of supplying food and other necessities "cannot even be attempted until there is in Hungary a Government which represents its people, and carries out in the letter and the spirit the engagements into which it has entered with the Associated Governments. . . . if peace is to be settled it can only be done with a Government which represents the Hungarian people and not with one that rests its authority upon terrorism."[7]

Six days later, on August 1, Bela Kun was overthrown. Whatever effect Hoover's message may have had on the Hungarian people, it was not repeated in the case of Russia. The food relief proposal for Russia was communicated through Fridtjof Nansen, a Norwegian polar explorer and national hero without political ties to either side, via radio broadcasts from the Eiffel Tower in Paris. One condition of the Nansen plan was that Allied agents should have the right to supervise distribution of the foodstuffs inside Russia. This left the Soviet leadership with an unpleasant choice: Lenin could fall in with what Hoover and Wilson anticipated would be a blow against Bolshevism, or he could take responsibility for depriving the Russian people of bread. The first meant surrendering authority over what are normally regarded as routine functions of governmental administration, the second breaking a promise the Bolsheviks had made in 1917, to give the people bread along with land and peace.

A second condition was that the Bolsheviks should agree to cease hostilities against their opponents inside R.ssia and pledge to stop their propangada against the institutions of other countries. Lenin replied that he was prepared to meet with representatives of the Allies to open "peace negotiations," but he could not stop fighting the "tools" of the Entente governments. "If left in peace and allowed free development Soviet Russia would soon be able to restore her national production, to regain her economic strength to provide for her own needs and to be helpful to other countries."[8]

Back To Siberia

The final sentences of Lenin's response to the Hoover-Nansen plan struck the Big Four at Versailles as a confession of weakness. French Premier Georges Clemenceau said that there was no doubt that Lenin's regime was on the decline. The French were impressed with the military progress Admiral Aleksandr Kolchak had been making against the Bolsheviks in Siberia. For his part Wilson wanted assurances that Kolchak, and any other group desiring aid, was prepared to work for an all-Russian government established on a "democratic basis."

On May 26, 1919, the Big Four decreed that Kolchak offered the best chance for the Russian people to resume control of their own affairs. The Allies announced their willingness to help him if, in return, he promised to convene a constitutional convention, hold free elections, bring Russia into the League of Nations, and assume the legal debts of former Russian governments. Kolchak's promissary note to that effect lost whatever value it might have had when his military fortunes deserted him. The admiral was caught and executed early in 1920. American troops were withdrawn from Siberia in April, because, as Lansing had written earlier to Wilson, "the Bolshevik army is approaching the region where our soldiers are, and contact with them will lead to open hostilities and to many complications. In other words, if we do not withdraw we shall have to wage war against the Bolsheviki."[9]

Having staked so much on the resurrection of the democratic spirit in Russia, Wilson continued his refusal to recognize what had materialized in the Bolshevik government. By this time Russia had become an issue in the domestic fight for ratification of the Versailles Treaty and entrance into the League of Nations. Progressive opponents of the league, led by Senator William E. Borah of Idaho, charged that the intervention was only the beginning of what would become a never-ending effort to maintain the status quo throughout the world. Soon Americans would be fighting to enforce French dictates against Germany, or Japanese demands on China. The league, charged Borah, was a compact among reactionary powers determined to enforce their will on the revolutionary, the defeated, and the weak.

Conservatives wanted out of Siberia, if only to prevent the growth of domestic radicalism. It was wrong to confuse the issues of intervention in some far off corner of the world, where it was sure to be ineffective, and the dangers of Communist propaganda at home. The intervention encouraged sympathy for the Bolsheviks—and by implication—for radicals everywhere. Wilson attempted to turn both Progressive fears and conservative apprehensions into arguments for the league during his crosscountry tour in the fall of 1919, but largely without success (see Document 31).

Wilson's health finally broke under the strain. As the "red scare" spread across the nation during the postarmistice era, wartime acts passed by Congress were enforced against presumed radicals and organized labor. The immediate cause of the "red scare" was the difficult readjustment to a peacetime economy, which produced a number of bitterly fought strikes. Returned veterans fought on both sides: unions against the American Legion. These industrial troubles seemed even more serious against the background of the Russian Revolution and Lenin's Marxist predictions. The National Association of Manufacturers declared solemnly—if partly for effect—that "unionism is nothing less than Bolshevism." As such it was "the greatest crime left in the world."

Real evidence of a radical conspiracy, however small, appeared in the outbreak of bombings against public figures. When one destroyed part of Attorney General A. Mitchell Palmer's home, the nation's chief law officer promised retaliation. What Palmer promised, he delivered. The "Palmer Raids" of December, 1919 and January, 1920, netted four thousand suspects, but no proven conspirators. Several hundred aliens were deported. But since the United States did not recognize any government in Russia, they could not be sent there. Finally it was decided to deposit the undesirables in Finland. Let them find their own way to the Communist utopia!

Physically disabled and sick at heart, the president sank back to the only position left to him: America must protect Russian territorial boundaries against marauders who sought to exploit its riches for their own advantage. The behavior of the nation's former allies in this regard seemed to Wilson decidely suspect. On more than one occasion during his last months in office he asked the State Department to investigate persistent reports of Anglo-French manipulations in Germany and Russia.

Whatever else was happening, it was certainly true that the British government had determined that the time had come to take a second look at the Russian situation by the end of 1919. Prime Minister David Lloyd George was saying that Europe might be a safer place for everyone if the Soviets could bring the civil war to a successful conclusion. They might well find that the problems involved in making Russia a going concern once again left little time or energy for foreign adventure. On November 8, 1919, the prime minister created something of a sensation with the observation that there could not be peace anywhere unless there was peace in Russia. A few days later he offered skeptics a second reason for coming to terms with the Bolsheviks, describing Russia as one of the world's great resources for food supplies and raw materials.

Lloyd George was much derided for his assertion that "the corn bins of Russia are bulging with grain," but the basic reasoning behind his grossly exaggerated estimates of Russian food supplies was not all that different from Hoover's emphasis on the importance of restarting production and distribution. To be sure, the prime minister gave it a more paradoxical twist: he hoped to use Russian grain to restore capitalism in Eastern and Central Europe.

Lloyd George followed these statements by urging the new Polish state to cease its hostilities against Russia, and by inviting Moscow to send a trade delegation to England. Negotiations continued for a month between the Soviet delegation and their British counterparts, leading to an agreement on July 7, 1920, to resume economic relations. In order to get this agreement, Lenin accepted three conditions: a cessation of hostile acts and propaganda outside Russia, the return of all prisoners of war, and recognition in principle of debts to private individuals. Though unprepared to enter into any agreements with Lenin, the United States also revoked the ban against private trading with the Bolsheviks on that same. But potential traders were warned that they could expect no assistance from American consuls or aid in facilitating credit arrangements.

Anglo-Russian economic relations did not develop satisfactorily despite Lloyd George's active interest. Trade expectations never really materialized. Bitter arguments developed over the issues of propaganda and debts, with charges of bad faith on both sides. These disagreements were cited by American opponents of recognition to argue that the only policy for the United States was to continue watchful waiting—and hoping. As a recent study of ideology and economics in the American response to Bolshevism ironically notes, "it appears quite probable that, if the United States had recognized only the small European portion of Russia actually controlled by the Bolsheviks in 1920 and if it had actively encouraged the establishment of non-Communist regimes elsewhere, the revolutionaries might ultimately have been deprived of valuable natural resources and might have been contained by a host of new, antipathetical neighbor states. By ideologically holding out for an entirely democratic, capitalistic Russia, the United States pursued a policy that resulted in the loss of the entire nation to Western political and economic traditions."[10]

No one in Wilson's narrowing circle of close advisers recommended such a policy. And whenever American exporters attempted to reopen contacts with Russian buyers, the State Department cast a baleful eye over the negotiations, usually enough to cause the offender to shrink back into conformity. Government witnesses testified to congressional committees that anyone who accepted Russian gold was in effect receiving stolen property— and would be liable for every penny once the Bolsheviks fell from power, which was as predictable as the law of gravity itself.

The task of restating American policy toward Russia in the last months of Wilson's term, when the president was too ill to take an active role, fell to his third secretary of state, Bainbridge Colby. Lansing had fallen out of favor for a number of reasons; his lack of enthusiasm for the league, a presumed desire to take charge of the government while Wilson lay ill in the White House, and, interestingly, for his willingness to consider military intervention against Mexico to bring that still unresolved situation to a successful conclusion. Colby defined the administration's attitude toward Bolshevik R. ssia one last time on August 10, 1920, in reply to an Italian inquiry about the Russo-Polish war. His note consisted of two essentials (which had not changed since the beginning): America opposed any "policy of dismember- ment" and was convinced that freed from outside pressure the Russians would themselves topple the tyranny that oppresses them. It was not quite true, of course, that Wilson had consistently refrained from using or supporting military force against the Bolsheviks, but he had always argued in Washington and in Paris that any attempt to check a revolutionary movement by means of deployed armies was like trying to use a broom to sweep back a high tide.

The Aftermath

"I do not fear Bolshevism," Wilson explained to a private interviewer on September 27, 1920, "but it must be resisted. Bolshevism is a mistake and it must be resisted as all mistakes must be resisted. If left alone, it will destroy itself. It cannot survive because it is wrong."[11] Wilson's stroke only served to strengthen those convictions, while it paralyzed American diplomacy gen- erally. The failure of the Senate to ratify the Versailles Treaty in a form acceptable to the president meant that the United States remained technically at war with the Central Powers while the rest of Europe attempted to come to terms with the postwar world. No progress had been made in settling the war debts/reparations question which prevented planners from mapping out an economic strategy for recovery.

America's relations with Japan and China, the latter just beginning a revolutionary stage which would continue for twenty-five years and cul- minate in a Communist victory in that country, had been left in an unsatisfactory state. A new government had replaced Carranza in Mexico, but the State Department demanded assurances from the regime concerning protection of American property in a form the Mexican leaders could not accept. In the 1920 compaign the Republicans promised a return to "normalcy" in domestic policy and an end to foreign crusades. Secretary of State Charles Evans Hughes then moved swiftly to complete a separate peace treaty with Germany and the other Central Powers, to set in motion a settlement with Mexico, and to initiate the lengthy negotiations which led to the Washington Naval Conference. But there was no diplomatic change toward Russia.

As in England, some interested American businessmen thought that trade was trade, even with Bolsheviks and should be pursued; a few hoped that economic contacts would lead to political relations. But the dominant groups among economic and political spokesmen rejected anything more than the most limited economic dealings for just those reasons. Secretary Hughes said only a few days after taking office in March, 1921, that the Soviets would have to meet certain basic conditions if they expected diplomatic recognition:

> If fundamental changes are contemplated, involving due regard for the protection of persons and property and the establishment of conditions essential to the maintenance of commerce, this Government will be glad to have convincing evidence of the consummation of such changes, and until this evidence is supplied this Government is unable to per- ceive that there is any proper basis for considering trade relations.[12]

Outside the ambit of regular diplomatic relations, Hoover, now secretary of commerce (and freed from Allied hinderances) renewed the offer of food relief for Russia's starving. In doing so he was at obvious crosspurposes with the Hughes view as stated above, specifically, that the Bolsheviks would have to stop being Communists if they expected American recognition and trade. But Hoover was a consistent Wilsonian: he fully believed that Bolshevism was a mistake and must be resisted, but the way to resist it was to give the people a viable alternative. Moreover, and again like Wilson, Hoover believed that America's competitors were hard at work to secure economic advantages and must not be allowed to capture the field. He reacted strongly, therefore, in December, 1921, when the secretary of state suggested that the government should encourage an expansion of German-Soviet trade in American products as the basis for informal and indirect economic relations.

Hoover's reply is commented on and explained by another historian of Russian-American relations, William Appleman Williams:

> Hoover's reference to the famine relief program that he also directed was of particular significance. "The relief measured," he explained to Hughes, "will build a situation which, combined with other factors, will enable the Americans to undertake the leadership in the reconstruction of Russia when the proper moment arrives." The Secretary of Commerce left no doubt as to his primary concern: "the hope of our commerce lies in the establishment of American firms abroad, distributing American goods under American direction; in the building of direct American financing and, above all, in the installation of American technology in Russian industries." Thus, once the Soviets were deposed—relations could be established only after "fundamental changes" were effected—did Hoover plan to replace Germany as the dominant influence in the Russian state.[13]

On a tactical level, Wilson's legacy was ambiguous, as the Hoover-Hughes dispute demonstrated. But shortly before his death the former president wrote a brief article, "The Road Away from Revolution." It was a fitting coda for a life spent searching for the highway to political and economic security within and between nations. More than in past utterances Wilson stressed that the Bolshevik revolution offered instruction to Americans, that "before we commit ourselves irreconcilably to an attitude of hostility to this movementof the time [anticapitalism], we ought frankly to put to ourselves the question, Is the capitalistic system unimpeachable?" (see Document 32).

Ten years later, Franklin Roosevelt moved to open economic and political relations with the Soviets because he, too, was seeking the road away from revolution and war. For some of his advisers the primary reason was to gain access to a supposedly growing market; for others the paramount factor was a desire to build a collective security system in the face of a new German-Japanese threat to world order. Still others wanted to damp down communist-capitalist antagonism in a time of economic crisis. None felt that any purpose was served by pretending to ignore the very existence of Communist Russia as a legitimate government.

"History" will not teach us if a different approach to the Bolsheviks in Wilson's time would have changed anything. It can help us to understand Woodrow Wilson and his time. It may suggest how decisions were shaped in the past, and the continuing impact these have upon our consciousness and understanding of today's events. The documents which follow may assist you to make your own judgments on some of these questions.

Notes

1. Wilson to Lansing, June 17, 1918, in, U.S. Department of State, *Papers Relating to the Foreign Relations of the United States: The Lansing Papers, 1914-1920*, 2 vols. (Washington, D.C.; Government Printing Office, 1940) II, 363.

2. George F. Kennan, *The Decision to Intervene* (Princeton: Princeton University Press, 1958), p. 404.

3. Betty Miller Unterberger, "President Wilson and the Decision to Send American Troops to Siberia," *Pacific Historical Review* 24 (February, 1955), pp. 63-74.

4. Lansing to Root, October 28, 1918, The Papers of Robert Lansing, Library of Congress, Washington, D.C.

5. Seymour, *Intimate Papers of Colonel House*, IV, 405.

6. Steffens, *The Autobiography of Lincoln Steffens* (New York: Harcourt, Brace, 1931), pp. 796-97.

7. Cited in Herbert Hoover, *The Ordeal of Woodrow Wilson* (New York: McGraw-Hill, 1958), pp. 137-38.

8. Lenin's reply dated May 14, 1919 is printed in, U.S. Department of State, *Papers Relating to the Foreign Relations of the United States, 1919: Russia* (Washington, D.C: Government Printing Office, 1937), pp. 111-15.

9. Lansing to Wilson, December 23, 1919, *Lansing Papers*, II, 392-93.

10. Joan Hoff Wilson, *Ideology and Economics: U.S. Relations with the Soviet Union, 1918-1933* (Columbia, Missouri: University of Missouri Press, 1974), p. 18.

11. Unpublished interview with Woodrow Wilson, September 27, 1920, in *Papers of Bainbridge Colby*, Library of Congress, Washington, D.C., Box 3B.

12. U.S. Department of State, *Papers Relating to the Foreign Relations of the United States, 1921*, vol. 2 (Washington: Government Printing Office, 1936), p. 768.

13. William Appleman Williams, *American-Russian Relations, 1781-1947* (New York: Rinehart & Co., 1952), p. 193.

part two

Documents of the Decision

1

Wilson as Politician

It is not difficult to find evidence of Woodrow Wilson's concern for a "party of conservative reform," but the speech he delivered to the Society of Virginians on November 30, 1904, in New York combines that concern with the future president's belief that southerners could lead the Democratic party back to national success against the special-interest dominated Republicans. Interesting also is the implication that "radicals" prevented the Democrats from achieving this goal earlier. Compare this speech with Lenin's words written about the same time on parliamentary democracy (Document 10).

Document†

The third annual dinner of the Society of the Virginians, given last evening at the Waldorf-Astoria, was one of the largest and one of the most successful reunions the society has held. More than 100 members of the society and invited guests sat at table. The speakers beginning with James W[addel]. Alexander, the Governor, as the president of the society is called, included President Woodrow Wilson of Princeton University, William B. Hornblower, F. Hopkinson Smith, and ex-Attorney General William A. Barber of South Carolina. Others who sat at the Governor's table were Vice.-Gov. H.R. Bayne, Col. A.G. Dickinson, Edward Owen, Robert L. Harrison and James A. Patterson. . . .

The feature of the evening was President Woodrow Wilsons speech, which was almost exclusively devoted to politics. President Wilson said that while it did not become him, as a person in an academic position such as he held, to discuss politics from a partisan point of view, he felt that he might well say something on general lines about matters affecting the country as a whole. He bagan with an incident of the campaign. He said:

Among my colleagues at Princeton is a son of James A. Garfield. Mr. Garfield came to me a little while before election and said: "They are asking me to go and make some political speeches. I did not know how it would impress you, and I thought I would ask you."

I told him that the only objection I had was that I was on the side against which he would speak, but that his being a member of the faculty of Princeton University did not destroy his privileges as an American citizen, and to go ahead and make all the speeches he wanted to. I do not believe it is the right thing for a Virginian to keep his mouth shut.

†From: New York *Sun*, No. 30, 1904, in *The Papers of Woodrow Wilson*, ed. Arthur S. Link (Princeton: Princeton University Press, 1973), vol. 15, pp. 545-49.

I feel that I am where I belong among you here. There was once a rather unsophisticated old woman who went to one of those side shows where they have marvellous pictures on the outside of things that are not to be seen on the inside. And in the show she saw a man who read a newspaper, or pretended to read a newspaper, through a two-inch plank.

"Come right along out of here, Silas," the old lady said to her hsuband. "This is no place for me with these thin clothes on!" (Prolonged laughter.)

Now, I have no such feelings here among you to-night. I feel that I am of you: that I belong here.

We Americans know a good deal, undoubtedly, about self-government. We understand each other when it comes to that subject. Yet, I fear we have not come to quite as free and cordial an understanding as we ought.

When we find out that all the best governed cities in the world are not American cities, it causes us to be "sickl[i]ed over with the pale cast of thought." I remember once, after a disaster at a municipal election here in New York, a gentleman was bemoaning to me the result, when it occurred to me to ask him if he had voted.

"Well, no," he replied, "I did not."

Then I replied that I did not see what he had to complain of; that he had done all he could to bring about the result that he much deplored.

Going on to discuss the political future of the South, President Wilson said:

No one can justly wonder at the present impatience of the Southern political leaders at finding themselves without real independence or influence in the politics of the country; the only section of the country which did not make a real choice of its political actions in the recent elections. But the only remedy suggested would put the Southern States in a still worse position.

To act independently of old party affiliations, as some of their leaders have recently proposed that they should act, would be to make them, if they still hung together and acted in concert, a third party in the politics of the country, and not a party of principle at that, but a geographical party, a sectional party, which would act in isolation and draw upon itself afresh old enmities and suspicions.

The real opportunity of the South is of another sort. It has now a unique opportunity to perform a great national service. As the only remaining part of the Democratic party that can command a majority of the votes in its constituencies, let the South demand a rehabilitation of the Democratic party on the only lines that can restore it to dignity and power.

Since 1896 the Democratic party has permitted its name to be used by men who ought never to have been admitted to its counsels, men who held principles and professed purposes which it had always hitherto repudiated.

By themselves and under their proper designation as populists and radical theorists, contemptuous alike of principle and of experience, these men could never have played any role in national politics but that of a noisy minority. Since they forced themselves into the councils of the party and got the use of its name, every doubtful State has been turned into an enthusiastic supporter of the Republican party. Until it has read them out of the party as an alien faction there will be no doubtful States again.

It is now high time that the South, which has endured most by way of humiliation at the hands of this faction, should demand that it be utterly and once for all thrust out of Democratic counsels; that the men of New York, New Jersey, Connecticut, Massachusetts, Indiana and the prosperous States beyond the Mississippi who wish for reform without loss of stability should join with it to reassert the principles and return to the practices of the historic party which has always stood for thoughtful moderation in affairs and a careful use of the powers of the Federal Government in the interest of the whole people of whatever class or occupation.

There is no longer any Democratic party either in the South or in any Northern State which the discredited radicals can use. The great body of one-time Democrats that musters strong enough to win elections has revolted and will act with no organization which harbors the radicals—as the radicals themselves did not in fact act with the organization they themselves had discredited in the recent campaign, when the whole country felt that the Democratic party was still without definite character or make-up.

The country, as it moves forward in its great material progress, needs and will tolerate no party of discontent or radical experiment; but it does need a party of conservative reform, acting in the spirit of law and of ancient institutions. Hosts of voters are waiting and ready to flock back to the standard of such a party when once they see it come upon the field properly purged and authenticated.

The old Democratic party stood by the South through good report and ill; the South has now an opportunity to requite its thankless services by recalling it to its old counsel and spirit. To do this would be to render a real national service conceived in the interest of the whole country of whatever opinion; for the politics of the nation cannot go normally and healthfully forward without the stimulation and contest of two parties of principle.

President Wilson's speech was greeted with one of the most remarkable demonstrations of approval that has been manifested at a public dinner in this city for a long time. He was time and again overwhelmed with applause as he was speaking and had to wait until the handclapping ceased long enough to permit his voice to be heard before he could go on. When he closed, in a voice impressive and earnest in its tone, the applause broke loose like a pent-up torrent, and he was called to his feet to bow his acknowledgements to the extraordinary ovation tendered him.

2

"Cooperation" with Latin America

Wilson's cautionary statement to America's neighbors in the hemisphere was expressed in rather self-righteous terms. Did his statement that there could be "no freedom without order" assume that all people wanted American-style freedom, and that they could achieve it without disorder? Such a blanket statement seemingly defined all revolutions as pointless—a surprisingly ahistorical attitude. In the light of the Mexican and Russian revolutions, Wilson modified some—but not all—of these views.

Document†

In view of questions which are naturally uppermost in the public mind just now, the President issued the following statement to the public, March 11, 1913.

"One of the chief objects of my administration will be to cultivate the friendship and deserve the confidence of our sister republics of Central and South America, and to promote in every proper and honorable way the interests which are common to the peoples of the two continents. I earnestly desire the most cordial understanding and cooperation between the peoples and leaders of America and, therefore, deem it my duty to make this brief statement.

"Cooperation is possible only when supported at every turn by the orderly processes of just government based upon law, not upon arbitrary or irregular force. We hold, as I am sure all thoughtful leaders of republican government everywhere hold, that just government rests always upon the consent of the governed, and that there can be no freedom without order based upon law and upon the public conscience and approval. We shall look to make these principles the basis of mutual intercourse, respect, and helpfulness between our sister republics and ourselves. We shall lend our influence of every kind to the realization of these principles in fact and practice, knowing that disorder, personal intrigues, and defiance of constitutional rights weaken and discredit government and injure none so much as the people who are unfortunate enough to have their common life and their common affairs so tainted and disturbed. We can have no sympathy with those who seek to seize the power of government to advance their own personal interests or ambition. We are

†From: Wilson to the American Diplomatic Officers in Latin America, March 12, 1913, in U.S., Department of State, *Papers Relating to the Foreign Relations of the United States, 1913*, (Washington, D.C.: Government Printing Office, 1920), p. 7.

the friends of peace, but we know that there can be no lasting or stable peace in such circumstances. As friends, therefore, we shall prefer those who are in the interest of peace and honor, who protect private rights, and respect the restraints of constitutional provision. Mutual respect seems to us the indispensable foundation of friendship between states, as between individuals.

"The United States has nothing to seek in Central and South America except the lasting interests of the peoples of the two continents, the security of governments intended for the people and for no special group or interest, and the development of personal and trade relationships between the two continents which shall rebound to the profit and advantage of both and interfere with the rights and liberties of neither."

From these principles may be read so much of the future policy of this Government as it is necessary now to forecast, and in the spirit of these principles I may, I hope, be permitted with as much confidence as earnestness to extend to the Governments of all the Republics of America the hand of genuine disinterested friendship, and to pledge my own honor and the honor of my colleagues to every enterprise of peace and amity that a fortunate future may disclose."

3

China and
the Bankers

The statement on China and the bankers established Wilson as anti-Wall Street in the minds of many Americans. But it reaffirmed the president's commitment to open door expansionism as well. Foreign nations could well be excused for confusing America's mission for manifest destiny, especially when the president's new ambassador to China made it clear that he was determined that American businessmen would compete vigorously in China.

Document†
Only for your information and guidance, I quote the following statement issued by the President:

"We are informed that at the request of the last administration a certain group of American bankers undertook to participate in the loan now desired by the Government of China (approximately $125,000,000). Our Government wished American bankers to participate along with the bankers of other nations, because it desired that the good will of the United States toward China should be exhibited in this practical way, that American capital should have access to that great country, and that the United States should be in a position to share with the other powers any political responsibilities that might be associated with the development of the foreign relations of China in connection with her industrial and commercial enterprises. The present administration has been asked by this group of bankers whether it would also request them to participate in the loan. The representatives of the bankers through whom the administration was approached declared that they would continue to seek their share of the loan under the proposed agreements only if expressly requested to do so by the Government. The administration has declined to make such request, because it did not approve the conditions of the loan or the implications of responsibility on its own part which it was plainly told would be involved in the request.

"The conditions of the loan seem to us to touch very nearly the administrative independence of China itself, and this administration does not feel that it ought, even by implication, to be a party to those conditions. The responsibility on its part which would be implied in requesting the bankers to undertake the loan might conceivably go the length in some unhappy contingency of forcible interference in the financial, and even the political, affairs of that great oriental State, just now awakening to a consciousness of

†From: The Acting Secretary of State to Certain American Diplomatic Officers, March 19, 1913, U.S., Department of State, in *Papers Relating to the Foreign Relations of the United States, 1913* (Washington, D.C.: Government Printing Office, 1920), pp. 170-71.

its power and of its obligations to its people. The conditions include not only the pledging of particular taxes, some of them antiquated and burdensome, to secure the loan, but also the administration of those taxes by foreign agents. The responsibility on the part of our Government implied in the encouragement of a loan thus secured and administered is plain enough and is obnoxious to the principles upon which the government of our people rests.

"The Government of the United States is not only willing, but earnestly desirous, of aiding the great Chinese people in every way that is consistent with their untrammled development and its own immemorial principles. The awakening of the people of China to a consciousness of their responsibilities under free government is the most significant, if not the most momentous, event of our generation. With this movement and aspiration the American people are in profound sympathy. They certainly wish to participate, and participate very generously, in the opening to the Chinese and to the use of the world the almost untouched and perhaps unrivaled resources of China.

"The Government of the United States is earnestly desirous of promoting the most extended and intimate trade relationship between this country and the Chinese Republic. The present administration will urge and support the legislative measures necessary to give American merchants, manufactuers, contractors, and engineers the banking and other financial facilities which they now lack and without which they are at a serious disadvantage as compared with their industrial and commercial rivals. This is its duty. This is the main material interest of its citizens in the development of China. Our interests are those of the open door—a door of friendship and mutual advantage. This is the only door we care to enter."

4

Justifying Intervention in Mexico

Linkage of the Mexican and Russian revolutions, and America's responsibility to each, became common following the Bolshevik Revolution. Note Wilson's references to the activities of German agents in Mexico. A similar rationale for intervention to restore the Russian revolution to the Russian people was taking shape in the president's mind even as he spoke to Mexican newspaper editors on June 7, 1918. Finally, note the president's comments on the Russian situation and the importance of "the foundations of established order" to enable Mexico to develop its resources. (See also Document 23 for the stated reasons for American intervention in Russia in 1918.)

Document†

I have never received a group of men who were more welcome than you are, because it has been one of my distresses during the period of my Presidency that the Mexican people did not more thoroughly understand the attitude of the United States towards Mexico. I think I can assure you, and I hope you have had every evidence of the truth of my assurance, that that attitude is one of sincere friendship. And not merely the sort of friendship which prompts one not to do his neighbor any harm, but the sort of friendship which earnestly desires to do his neighbor service.

My own policy, the policy of my own administration, towards Mexico was at every point based upon this principle, that the internal settlement of the affairs of Mexico was none of our business; that we had no right to interfere with or to dictate to Mexico in any particular with regard to her own affairs. Take one aspect of our relations which at one time may have been difficult for you to understand: When we sent troops into Mexico, our sincere desire was nothing else than to assist you to get rid of a man who was making the settlement of your affairs for the time being impossible. We had no desire to use our troops for any other purpose, and I was in hopes that by assisting in that way and then immediately withdrawing I might give substantial proof of the truth of the assurances that I had given your Government through President Carranza.

And at the present time it distresses me to learn that certain influences which I assume to be German in their origin are trying to make a wrong

†From: Wilson, "An Address to a Party of Mexican Editors," June 7, 1918, Official U.S. Bulletin No. 332, in *The Public Papers of Woodrow Wilson*, eds. Ray Stannard Baker and William E. Dodd (New York: Harper & Bros., 1927), vol. 5, pp. 223-28.

impression throughout Mexico as to the purposes of the United States, and not only a wrong impression, but to give an absolutely untrue account of things that happen. You know the distressing things that have been happening just off our coasts. You know of the vessels that have been sunk. I yesterday received a quotation from a paper in Guadlajara which stated that thirteen of our battleships had been sunk off the capes of the Chesapeake. You see how dreadful it is to have people so radically misinformed. It was added that our Navy Department was withholding the truth with regard to these sinkings. I have no doubt that the publisher of the paper published that in perfect innocence without intending to convey wrong impressions, but it is evident that allegations of that sort proceed from those who wish to make trouble between Mexico and the United States.

Now, gentlemen, for the time being at any rate—and I hope it will not be a short time—the influence of the United States is somewhat pervasive in the affairs of the world, and I believe that it is pervasive because the nations of the world which are less powerful than some of the greatest nations are coming to believe that our sincere desire is to do disinterested service. We are the champions of those nations which have not had a military standing which would enable them to compete with the strongest nations in the world, and I look forward with pride to the time, which I hope will soon come, when we can given substantial evidence, not only that we do not want anything out of this war, but that we would not accept anything out of it, that it is absolutely a case of disinterested action. And if you will watch the attitude of our people, you will see that nothing stirs them so deeply as assurances that this war, so far as we are concerned, is for idealistic objects. One of the difficulties that I experienced during the first three years of the war—the years when the United States was not in the war—was in getting the foreign offices of European nations to believe that the United States was seeking nothing for herself, that her neutrality was not selfish, and that if she came in, she would not come in to get anything substantial out of the war, any material object, any territory, or trade, or anything else of that sort. In some of the foreign offices there were men who personally knew me and they believed, I hope, that I was sincere in assuring them that our purposes were disinterested, but they thought that these assurances came from an academic gentleman removed from the ordinary sources of information and speaking the idealistic purposes of the cloister. They did not believe that I was speaking the real heart of the American people, and I knew all along that I was. Now I believe that everybody who comes into contact with the American people knows that I am speaking their purposes.

The other night in New York, at the opening of the campaign for funds for our Red Cross, I made an address. I had not intended to refer to Russia, but I was speaking without notes and in the course of what I said my thought was led to Russia, and I said that we meant to stand by Russia just as firmly as we would stand by France or England or any other of the Allies. The audience to which I was speaking was not an audience from which I would have expected an enthusiastic response to that. It was rather too well dressed. It was not an audience, in other words, made of the class of people whom you would suppose to have the most intimate feeling for the sufferings of the ordinary man in Russia, but that audience jumped into the aisles, the whole audience rose to its feet, and nothing that I had said on that occasion aroused anything like the enthusiasm that that single sentence aroused. Now, there is a sample, gentlemen. We cannot make anything out of Russia. We cannot make anything out of standing by Russia at this time—the most remote of the European nations, so far as we are concerned, the one with which we have had the least connections in trade and advantage—and yet the people of the United States rose to that suggestion as to no other that I made in that address. That is the heart of America, and we are ready to show you by any act of friendship that you may propose our real feelings toward Mexico.

Some of us, if I may say so privately, look back with regret upon some of the more ancient relations that we have had with Mexico long before our generation; and America, if I may so express it, would now feel ashamed to take advantage of a neighbor. So I hope that you can carry back to your homes something better than the assurances of words. You have had contact with our people. You know your own personal reception. You know how gladly we have opened to you the doors of every establishment that you wanted to see and have shown you just what we were doing, and I hope you have gained the right impression as to why we were doing it. We are doing it, gentlemen, so that the world may never hereafter have to fear the only thing that any nation has to dread, the unjust and selfish aggression of another nation. Some time ago, as you probably all know, I proposed a sort of Pan-American agreement. I had perceived that one of the difficulties of our relationship with Latin America was this: The famous Monroe Doctrine was adopted without your consent, without the consent of any of the Central or South American States.

If I may express it in the terms that we so often use in this country, we said, "We are going to be your big brother, whether you want us to be or not." We did not ask whether it was agreeable to you that we should be your big brother. We said we were going to be. Now, that was all very well so far as protecting you from aggression from the other side of the water was concerned, but there was nothing in it that protected you from aggression from us, and I have repeatedly seen the uneasy feeling on the part of representatives of the states of Central and South America that our self-appointed protection might be for our own benefit and our own interests and not for the interest of our neighbors. So I said, "Very well, let us make an arrangement by which we will give bond. Let us have a common guarantee, that all of us will sign, of political independence and territorial integrity. Let us agree that if any one of us, the United States included, violates the political independence or the territorial integrity of any of the others, all the others will jump on her." I pointed out to some of the gentlemen who were less inclined to enter into this arrangement than others that that was in effect giving bonds on the part of the United States, that we would enter into an arrangement by which you would be protected from us.

Now, that is the kind of agreement that will have to be the foundation of the future life of the nations of the world, gnetlemen. The whole family of nations will have to guarantee to each nation that no nation shall violate its political independence or its territorial integrity. That is the basis, the only conceivable basis, for the future peace of the world, and I must admit that I was ambitious to have the states of the two continents of America show the way to the rest of the world as to how to make a basis of peace. Peace can come only by trust. As long as there is suspicion there is going to be misunderstanding, and as long as there is misunderstanding there is going to be trouble. If you can once get a situation of trust then you have got a situation of permanent peace. Therefore, everyone of us, it seems to me, owes it as a patriotic duty to his own country to plant the seeds of trust and of confidence instead of the seeds of suspicion and variety of interest. That is the reason that I began by saying to you that I have not had the pleasure of meeting a group of men who were more welcome than you are, because you are our near neighbors. Suspicion on your part or misunderstanding on your part distresses us more than we would be distressed by similar feelings on the part of those less nearby.

When you reflect how wonderful a storehouse of treasure Mexico is, you can see how her future must depend upon peace and honor, so that nobody shall exploit her. It must depend upon every nation that has any relations with her, and the citizens of any nation that has relations with her, keeping within the bounds of honor and fair dealing and justice, because so soon as you can admit your own capital and the capital of the world to the free use of the resources of Mexico, it will be one of the most wonderfully rich and prosperous countries in the world. And when you have the foundations of established order, and the world has come to its senses again, we shall, I hope, have the very best connections that will assure us all a permanent cordiality and friendship.

5

Russia and the Bankers

Ambassador David R. Francis's first reports from Russia in May, 1916, reflected his disappointment at the lukewarm welcome American commercial overtures had received, and his chagrin at Allied diplomacy toward that country. American suspicions of Anglo-French motivations antedated 1917 and continued (in fact deepened) in the revolutionary period. Obviously, Wilson could not reorganize the world along liberal lines if the Allies insisted upon building up economic blocs for the postwar period, nor could American commerce get its fair share of the Russian trade.

Document†

Petrograd, *undated.*
[Received May 2, 1916—8:15 a. m.]

Took charge 28th on arrival. Dearing [counselor of embassy] had arranged with Foreign Office initial informal visits with Minister of Foreign Affairs and President Council of Ministers. Latter received me 3 o'clock afternoon 29th. He received me cordially; we exchanged views freely concerning relations between our countries, each expressing desire to promote existing friendly feeling. I expressed a desire and intention actively to endeavor to establish and foster direct commercial relations between the two countries without any intermediary whatever, in which he heartily concurred. Called on Sazonoff 6 o'clock, being accompanied by Dearing in both visits. Had conference hour and 20 minutes with Sazonoff, who was cordial, courteous, attentive, candid, responsive, but surprised me immeasurably when he said with the [apparent omission] positiveness that no commercial treaty can now be negotiated. I called his attention to Marye's [Francis's predecessor in Russia] report that Russia had been awaiting advances from us for negotiating new treaties and expressed willingness and desire therefor. He admitted so telling Marye but said that was 6 months ago and subject was never broached again by Marye, that too late now because Allies had called an economic conference for June 1st Paris, and Russia will negotiate no commercial conventions with any country before that conference. He intimated that such conference might determine to establish different commercial relations with Allies, with friendly countries and with belligerents. He also insinuated that when commercial treaty is negotiated it would specially export [*sic*] to those countries which extend like favors to Russia in import duties. He furthermore

†From: Francis to Robert Lansing, 1916, in U.S., Department of State, *Papers Relating to the Foreign Relations of the United States: The Lansing Papers, 1914-1920* (Washington, D.C.: Government Printing.Office, 1940), vol. 2, pp. 309-12.

stated in good spirit that the denouncing by us of the treaty of 1832 had created no resentment in Russia and had not interfered with the trade between the countries which he said would continue, he trusted, in the future as in the past. I said his position was surprising and disappointing to me to a degree and ventured further the statement that the principal object of my appointment as advised by yourself and President Wilson was to negotiate treaty on commerce and navigation. Attempted to impress him with friendly interest in Russia now cherished by our people with our appreciation of Russia's manifestations of good will in the past and with expressed desire by our commercial classes to foster Russian commerce. He expressed gratification at such statements but remained firm in refusing consideration of the commercial treaty certainly until after the Allied conference at which Russia will be represented by comptroller of the Empire and four other potential [*sic*] officials. Expressed hope that my ambassadorial mission would prove agreeable and interesting and smilingly said duties of position would be sufficiently onerous without negotiating treaty. Said had heard rumor that my appointment was influenced by German sympathy and had questioned Bakhmeteff thereon but Bakhmeteff's reply said such rumor groundless and consequently Government here wholly uninfluenced by rumor which he did not credit. Returned to Embassy at 7:30 p.m., and immediately sent a note to Sazonoff as per arrangement asking when Emperor would receive me. Sazonoff forwarded same to Emperor immediately and am expecting reply to-day. Hope Emperor will receive me before returning to front but if so such action will be almost unprecedently prompt. Sazonoff in conference with Dearing March 30th expressed no opposition to negotiations commercial treaty although Dearing says that cannot recall that he definitely expressed willingness therefor, while expressing disappointment that Marye's negotiations had not been carried further. Consequently conclude Sazonoff's opposition is the result of recent conferences with Allies. Respectfully suggest I have lost no time since arrival morning 28th.

Francis

Petrograd, *May 2, 1916.*
[Received June 1.]

My Dear Mr. Secretary: I cabled you Sunday of my arrival and of my taking charge on April 28, and of sending a note on the same day to the Foreign Office and of my conference with the Minister of Foreign Affairs and also with the President of the Council of Ministers. My conferences with both of these officials was set forth almost in detail in the cablegram: consequently I shall not tire your patience in a résumé further than to say that the statement of Mr. Sazonoff was so surprising and inexplicable to me that I have been endeavoring since the interview to ascertain the cause for this change of position or of policy on the part of Russia toward the United States in regard to a commercial treaty.

I wrote you at length twice on the steamer while en route from New York to Christiania, and in both letters expressed my fear that certain interests in

New York were making effort to have all trade between our country and Russia pay tribute to England as an intermediary. Since arriving here my fears have not been dissipated; in fact I have heard many things which confirm the suspicions I have cherished.

The economic conference between the Allies which is fixed for Paris June first was, in my judgment, inspired by England, as that country is making decided effort to occupy toward Russia the position held by Germany before the war. It is true that both Sazonoff and Sturmer expressed themselves as favoring direct commercial relations between their country and ours, but the English influence here is very strong and a persistent effort is being made to strengthen it. The loan which was being negotiated in New York some eight weeks ago, but for some unaccountable reason has not been consummated, was alluded to by Sazonoff in my interview with him, and he expressed the opinion that it would be impossible for America to get what he called double security on any loan our banks might make to Russia. When I asked him what he meant by double security he said that our capitalists were demanding in addition to the obligation specific collateral. I told him that no country now engaged in war would be able to negotiate a loan in America without collateral and cited my experience and that of others with the Anglo-French loan which we were unable to sell at 98, as we endeavored to do; and in fact never since the expiration of the syndicate have we been able to dispose of those securities without loss. From 96 1/4 it declined to 93 5/8, and when I left America was selling at 95. All of this I told Mr. Sazonoff, but he persisted in saying that Russia would make no loan that required any security otherpersisted in saying that Russia would make no loan that required any security other than the faith or credit of the government itself.

In talking with Mr. Meserve, a representative of the National City Bank, on Saturday he tole me that Russia had agreed, or was about to agree early in March, to the requirements of New York bankers, but subsequently refused to do so, and the only way of accounting for the change in position was the influence of England which was desirous that all foreign relations of a commercial or financial character had by Russia should be through London.

In a talk with a gentleman today who has had a great deal of experience in Russia and is well known in the United States, the opinion was expressed that Bark, who is the Minister of Finance of Russia, is completely under British influence, and the same gentleman went so far as to state that in his judgment Sazonoff is held in the position of Minister of Foreign Affairs by British rather than by Russian support. If this is true, and I am not prepared to question it, we can account for Russia's change of front concerning the commercial treaty with the United States.

Mr. Sazonoff seemed to be prepared for my broaching the subject of a commercial treaty, because when I did so he very promptly stated that Russia would make no commercial treaty now with any country whatever. In addition to expressing sincere disappointment on the part of our government and our people generally, I made effort to impress upon Mr. Sazonoff that personally I so regretted his position that if not discouraged I was greatly chagrined because of the apparent impossibility of achieving what was my main object in accepting the Russian mission. Our interview was in good spirit on both sides, but there was no variation in his expression to the effect that nothing certainly would be considered until after the Paris conference.

6

War Message, 1917

Wilson's war message made it plain that the president went into that conflict determined to bring out of the horror and confusion of war a new order. In some ways it was a three-sided conflict: Germany and the Central Powers, England and France and their Allies, and the United States. Now Russia had joined the United States—or so it was hoped and/or feared. No longer would the Allies be able to plan on restoring the old political or economic order. Note finally the reuse of the German "agent" theory in regard to the Mexican situation.

Document†

A steadfast concert for peace can never be maintained except by a partnership of democratic nations. No autocratic government could be trusted to keep faith within it or observe its covenants. It must be a league of honor, a partnership of opinion. Intrigue would eat its vitals away; the plottings of inner circles who could plan what they would and render account to no one would be a corruption seated at its very heart. Only free peoples can hold their purpose and their honor steady to a common end and prefer the interests of mankind to any narrow interest of their own.

Does not every American feel that assurance has been added to our hope for the future peace of the world by the wonderful and heartening things that have been happening within the last few weeks in Russia? Russia was known by those who knew it best to have been always in fact democratic at heart, in all the vital habits of her thought, in all the intimate relationships of her people that spoke their natural instinct, their habitual attitude towards life. The autocracy that crowned the summit of her political structure, long as it had stood and terrible as was the reality of its power, was not in fact Russian in origin, character, or purpose; and now it has been shaken off and the great, generous Russian people have been added in all their naïve majesty and might to the forces that are fighting for freedom in the world, for justice, and for peace. Here is a fit partner for a League of Honor.

One of the things that has served to convince us that the Prussian autocracy was not and could never be our friend is that from the very outset of the present war it has filled our unsuspecting communities and even our offices of government with spies and set criminal intrigues everywhere afoot against our national unity of counsel, our peace within and without, our industries and our commerce. Indeed, it is now evident that its spies were

†From: Wilson, War Message to Congress, April 2, 1917, in *The Public Papers of Woodrow Wilson*, eds. Dodd and Baker, vol. 5, pp. 12-13.

here even before the war began; and it is unhappily not a matter of conjecture but a fact proved in our courts of justice that the intrigues which have more than once come perilously near to disturbing the peace and dislocating the industries of the country have been carried on at the instigation, with the support, and even under the personal direction of official agents of the Imperial Government accredited to the Government of the United States. Even in checking these things and trying to extirpate them we have sought to put the most generous interpretation possible upon them because we knew that their source lay not in any hostile feeling or purpose of the German people towards us (who were no doubt as ignorant of them as we ourselves were), but only in the selfish designs of a Government that did what it pleased and told its people nothing. But they have played their part in serving to convince us at last that that Government entertains no real friendship for us and means to act against our peace and security at its convenience. That it means to stir up enemies against us at our very doors the intercepted note to the German Minister at Mexico City is eloquent evidence.

7

Preserving and Strengthening Russian Morale

Wilson's faith in public diplomacy was not a personal obsession; American policy makers since the time of their own revolution against great Britain and the ways of old world diplomacy, have expressed convictions similar to those stated in this report by the Root Mission. Publicizing American war aims was immediately thought of as the best way to combat German influences, which, in turn were thought to be behind Bolshevik agitation against the Provisional Government. It took a good deal of optimism, however, to assume that an American advertising man or two hundred YMCA men could turn around the deteriorating situation in Russia.

Document†

*Supplementary Report of the Special Diplomatic Mission to Russia
to the Secretary of State*
[Extract]
PLANS FOR AMERICAN COOPERATION TO PRESERVE AND
STRENGTHEN THE MORALE OF THE CIVIL POPULATION
AND THE ARMY OF RUSSIA

I. PLAN TO PROMOTE AN EDUCATIONAL CAMPAIGN

1. AIM
To influence the attitude of the people of Russia for the prosecution of the war as the only way of perpetuating their democracy.

2. CONSIDERATIONS EMPHASIZING THE IMPORTANCE
OF SUCH A CAMPAIGN
Germany has been and waging an able propaganda in Russia to weaken and destroy the fighting spirit of the people. We found evidences that this effort is

†From: U.S., Department of State, *Papers Relating to The Foreign Relations of The United States, 1918: Russia* (Washington, D.C.: Government Printing Office, 1931), vol. 1, pp. 147-53.

generously financed, that it is conducted on a large scale, and that it has been most effective. It can be counteracted and overcome only by means of an adequate campaign of education.

There is in operation in Russia to-day no really adequate plan designed to counteract the efforts put forth by Germany to poison opinion and to paralyze action. There are commendable efforts both on the part of individual Russians and of certain of the Allies but none of these activities singly or all of them combined are capable of meeting the need.

We came to the conclusion, after examining all that is being done, that if the situation is to be met and met in time the United States must take the matter in hand. America has the necessary resources. America has evolved the most effective methods. America has available men trained for such educational work.

There has been no time when American cooperation in this sphere would count so much in Russia as the present. Owing to the prompt initiative of President Wilson in recognizing the Provisional Government and owing to the visit and the work accomplished by the Special Diplomatic Mission, America just now has most favorable access to Russia. Russia is ready to listen to America, and is eager to learn from her. Moreover, the present is incomparably the most critical period from a military point of view. The liberties of Russia—all that the Russian revolution has made possible—are endangered by Germany.

From the point of view of winning the war, it is vitally important that Russia be kept in the war, and, to this end, that her people shall be led to realize vividly what is at stake, and that they shall be inspired with hope in the successful outcome of the struggle. If, through our failure to keep alive the interest of the Russian people and to maintain among them a realizing sense of the significance of the sacrifices already made, Russia should lose heart and virtually be eliminated from the war, the consequences will be most serious.

Russia is possibly the most isolated nation among all the Allies. This is due to her geographical position and the very poor means of communication with the outside world. It takes a longer time to receiver letters and periodicals in Russia from the other Allies than is the case with any other Allied country. Moreover, the Russian press has the most meager and unsatisfactory foreign cable service. Germany has so clouded the waters of the press in the Scandinavian countries that little light of the kind most needed comes from Russia's nearest and most accessible neighbors.

The plans we propose call for an expenditure the first year of approximately $5,500,000. Members of our mission were told by those who are in a position to estimate facts that Germany has spent in her propaganda of intrigue in Russia since the revolution 48,000,000 rubles, or $3,000,000 a month. It is estimated that it costs the Allies $10,000,000 to keep one regiment one year at the front. The proposed campaign of education is directed to helping to develop a spirit which will hold on the eastern front 640 regiments of over 3,000 men each. The combined daily expenditures of the Allies have amounted to over $75,000,000. This vast outlay is devoted almost exclusively to providing for the *material* factors essential to the proper prosecution of the war. Is it not desirable to devote the relatively small sum suggested to insure the larger conservation and exercise of the *moral* factor in that area of the war where the situation is so critical?

America, as well as Russia, has much at stake. If Russia can be helped to hold her armies in being and to keep her men in the trenches, it will make it necessary that the enemy countries maintain on the eastern front over 140 divisions of troops. This has a most direct bearing on the extent of the exertions and sacrifices of America in the war.

The Russian civil and military authorities assured us that they would welcome and give every facility to any efforts which America might put forth in the direction of wise educational effort.

3. PRINCIPAL MEANS OR METHODS TO BE EMPLOYED

(*a*) Establishment of a modern news service designed to furnish news to all periodicals throughout Russia. This agency would specialize on American news. Nothing corresponding to this now exists. It would be necessary to have in Petrograd an American general manager and two American assistants to select the news from America and in Russia to be used, a worker in America to gather and forward the right kind of American news, a staff of five Russian writers and translators, also an efficient office force.

(*b*) Large use of effective pamphlets and leaflets. There is no land in the world where the thirst for literature dealing with current questions is greater to-day than it is in Russia. This is, of course, due to the revolution. Among those who can read there is only one activity which is more in evidence, and that is talking. Large use should be made of pictures or illustrations in connection with the new printed matter. Arrangements should be made with the news kiosks throughout the country to slip these leaflets into all papers sold.

(*c*) A well-managed film service would also accomplish in Russia more than in any other land. The experience of the British has pointed the way to a wide use of this means. The following classes of films should be prepared and used: war films; films of American life in the country, in manufacturing centers, and in commerce; American comic films; and above all, film stories of a patriotic character and especially illustrating the struggle for democracy. For the proper handling of this agency there would be needed an American manager and an assistant, also at least five well-qualified traveling men to introduce and supervise (not operate) the service. They would see that all centers are supplied with news films.

(*d*) Special advertising, particularly by means of illustrated colored posters, is a means well fitted for Russia. Experience in connection with floating their different loans confirms the usefulness of this plan. To accomplish the best results there should be in charge an expert American advertising man with a good assistant.

(e The most popular method for influencing Russian opinion is that of speech. Therefore, large use should be made of well-qualified speakers or teachers. Why should there not be a carefully selected body of hundreds of able Russians going as teachers about the towns and villages as well as among the millions of men under arms? These speakers or teachers could be brought together in large groups or companies for the purpose of preparation for their work and of unifying its impact.

II. PLAN TO STRENGTHEN THE MORALE OF THE ARMY—IMPORTANCE; PRACTICABILITY AND URGENCY OF THIS UNDERTAKING

Russia has called to the colors since the war began not less than 13,200,000 men. This constitutes the largest army assembled by any one nation in the history of the world. Of this vast number it is estimated that fully 2,000,000 have already been killed or have died as the result of wounds or diseases occasioned by the war. Another 2,000,000 are to-day prisoners of war in Germany, Austria-Hungary, Bulgaria, and Turkey. Another 2,000,000 may be classified as permanently ineffective, chiefly those who have been seriously mutilated in warfare or shattered by disease. This leaves 7,200,000 men as comprising the total strength of the Russian army of to-day. Some authorities whom we consulted give a somewhat lower figure, but more would place it even higher. Of this army of to-day probably 2,100,000 are to be found in the seventy corps on the European front and the five on the Asiatic front; 1,000,000 in the depots or reserves; 1,000,000 in connection with garrisons and communications—thus leaving a little over 3,000,000 in training, on leave, or otherwise not immediately available for military operations, but potentially a most important asset. On this vast host of Russian men and boys rests the tremendous responsibility of maintaining and pressing the war on the long-drawn-out eastern front. The effectiveness and faithfulness with which they perform this critical duty will determine, far more largely than we in America have realized, the extent of the exertions and sacrifices, and the laying down of life and substance, of the American people in connection with the great struggle. Whatever can be done, therefore, to insure and develop the highest working efficiency and truly triumphant spirit of the Russian soldiers has a most direct, practical, and vital bearing on the destiny of America and the other Allies.

That there is imperative need of instituting measures for rendering practical service to the millions of Russian men and boys under arms or in uniform there can be no question in the mind of any one who has first-hand knowledge of conditions. This need existed before the Russian revolution. A similar need had been recognized in all the other Allied armies, and with greater or less thoroughness was being met; but, notwithstanding the most helpful activities of such agencies as the Zemstvo unions, there has been lacking in the Russian army from the beginning an agency to specialize on the physical, mental, social, and moral betterment of the men as has been done in so many of other countries by the Young Men's Christian Association. The Russian revolution has greatly accentuated the need. From the nature of the case the minds of multitudes of Russian soldiers have been more or less absorbed with the political and social issues thrust upon them by the revolution. Moreover, the subtle, able forces of German intrigue have taken advantage of these unsettled conditions and have waged a really masterly propaganda among large numbers of the troops in the garrisons, in the training camps, and, to a larger degree than might be thought possible, at the front. As one studies these troops wherever they are congregated throughout Russia or Siberia, at the front or at the base, one is impressed by the vast numbers who either are not occupied at all with activities related to the war or are devoting themselves to aimless and unprofitable political discussion. The practical problem, stated in a sentence, is: Shall these millions of young men and boys in garrisons, in reserve camps, and at the fighting front spend the five or more leisure hours which they have each day in idleness or in unprofitable or weakening agitation, or shall they devote these spare hours to healthful physical and social recreation, growth in knowledge and working efficiency, and unselfish service to their fellowmen? This war has shown the supreme importance of morale. Napoleon went so far as to maintain that morale counts for an army as three to one. How important it is that everything possible be done during these coming months to improve the morale, to strengthen the discipline, and to raise the spirit of our comrades in Russia.

The marvelous success achieved by the Young Men's Christian Association in the British, Canadian, and Australasian armies not only on the west front, but also in Egypt, Mesopotamia, Saloniki, and on the Gallipoli Peninsula, in the wonderful French army, as well as in the newly forming American army, has demonstrated the adaptability of this organization for meeting the situation in Russia. We are glad to state that even before we arrived in Russia some of the American Association secretaries, who have long been at work there in the prisoner-of-war camps, had become so impressed by the need and by the urgency of the situation that they, without knowledge of each other's action, had already inaugurated work among the Russian soldiers at a number of points as widely separated as Petrograd on the west, Tomsk and Irkutsk in Siberia, and Tashkent in Turkestan. These efforts met with the instant and enthusiastic approval of both soldiers and officers. To promote recreation and the physical conditioning of the men, football, volley ball, track athletics, relay races, and aquatics had been introduced. The educational work included language schools, courses for other useful studies, libraries, reading rooms, lectures, and moving picture shows. Wise use was being made of high-grade theatrical plays. The musical features of the work were also most welcome. The moral life of the soldiers received sympathetic and careful attention. Wherever possible, the men were being enlisted in unselfish service among their fellows. As we studied these experiments we asked ourselves the question, Why is not this work reproducible throughout the entire Russian army?

. . . All our investigations convinced us that the soldiers of Russia present to America possibly the largest single opportunity to help which has come to us during the war. Here is a field that stretches one-third of the way around the world. It involves literally millions of men and boys—nearly as many as to-day are serving in the combined armies of Britain, Canada, America, and France. It is wide open to our friendly approach. It is a most responsive field. At many points the Russian army reminded us quite as much of older boys as of mature men, and these hosts of boys, and the men too for that matter, can be led anywhere by workers of warm hearts, wise heads, and unselfish spirit. They are most responsive to kindness. Very many of them are eager for self-development and are truly idealistic. To deal in any worthy or adequate way with this boundless opportunity means that we must send over to Russia as soon as possible at least two hundred of the best qualified workers whom we can find. The difficulties which await these workers are so subtle and serious that we should send only men of established character, of rich experience, and of undiscourageable enthusiasm. It may be found wise and practicable to establish a language school where all of these workers can spend at least a short period on arriving in Russia, although a man should begin his study of the Russian language the day he decides to enter this field. For every American secretary there should be two or more Russian workers.

It would be difficult to overstate the urgency of this extraordinary situation. The late autumn and the winter months will constitute the most critical testing period. If these men can be afforded pleasant and profitable occupation during this trying time it will insure conservation of probably the greatest single asset of the Allied cause; whereas, if through the influence of counter-revolutionary forces, of German intrigue, and of disintegrating habits of dissipation and idleness, the great Russian army should be permitted to dissolve or be riven with seams of weakness, the most disastrous consequences will follow. Just now America, as no other nation, holds the key to the situation. Her prompt recognition of the revolutionary government and her genuine and expressed desire to do anything in her power to help Russia, make the Russian people peculiarly hospitable to American ideas and workers
. . . .

8 ═══════════════════════

═══════════════════ "Friendship
of the
American
People for
the People
of Russia"

Wilson was prepared to do his share to boost the Russian war effort and the Provisional Government. In this message to the Russian people he anticipated the Root Mission's report. The effort to balance encouragement and warning was typical of American (and Allied) policy toward the Provisional Government.

Document†

In view of the approaching visit of the American delegation to Russia to express the deep friendship of the American people for the people of Russia and to discuss the best and most practical means of coöperation between the two peoples in carrying the present struggle for the freedom of all peoples to a successful consummation, it seems opportune and appropriate that I should state again, in the light of this new partnership, the objects the United States has had in mind in entering the war. Those objects have been very much beclouded during the past few weeks by mistaken and misleading statements, and the issues at stake are too momentous, too tremendous, too significant, for the whole human race to permit any misinterpretations or misunderstandings, however slight, to remain uncorrected for a moment.

The war has begun to go against Germany, and in their desperate desire to escape the inevitable ultimate defeat, those who are in authority in Germany are using every possible instrumentality, are making use even of the influence of groups and parties among their own subjects to whom they have never been just or fair, or even tolerant, to promote a propaganda on both sides of the sea which will preserve for them their influence at home and their power abroad, to the undoing of the very men they are using.

The position of America in this war is so clearly avowed that no man can be excused for mistaking it. She seeks no material profit or aggrandizement of

†From: Wilson, "Friendship of The American People . . .," May 26, 1917, Official Bulletin No. 26, in *The Public Papers of Woodrow Wilson*, eds. Dodd and Baker, vol. 5, pp. 49-51.

any kind. She is fighting for no advantage or selfish object of her own, but for the liberation of peoples everywhere from the aggressions of autocratic force.

The ruling classes in Germany have begun of late to profess a like liberality and justice of purpose, but only to preserve the power they have set up in Germany and the selfish advantages which they have wrongly gained for themselves and their private projects of power all the way from Berlin to Bagdad and beyond. Government after Government has by their influence, without open conquest of its territory, been linked together in a net of intrigue directed against nothing less than the peace and liberty of the world. The meshes of that intrigue must be broken, but cannot be broken unless wrongs already done are undone, and adequate measures must be taken to prevent it from ever again being rewoven or repaired.

Of course, the Imperial German Government and those whom it is using for their own undoing are seeking to obtain pledges that the war will end in the restoration of the *status quo ante*. It was the *status quo ante* out of which this iniquitous war issued forth, the power of the Imperial German Government within the Empire and its widespread domination and influence outside of that Empire. That status must be altered in such fashion as to prevent any such hideous thing from ever happening again.

We are fighting for the liberty, the self-government, and the undictated development of all peoples, and every feature of the settlement that concludes this war must be conceived and executed for that purpose. Wrongs must first be righted and then adequate safeguards must be created to prevent their being committed again. We ought not to consider remedies merely because they have a pleasing and sonorous sound. Practical questions can be settled only by practical means. Phrases will not accomplish the result. Effective readjustments will, and whatever readjustments are necessary must be made.

But they must follow a principle and that principle is plain. No people must be forced under sovereignty under which it does not wish to live. No territory must change hands except for the purpose of securing those who inhabit it a fair chance of life and liberty. No indemnities must be insisted on except those that constitute payment for manifest wrongs done. No readjustments for power must be made except such as will tend to secure the future peace of the world and the future welfare and happiness of its peoples.

And then the free peoples of the world must draw together in some common covenant, some genuine and practical cooperation that will in effect combine their force to secure peace and justice in the dealings of nations with one another.

The brotherhood of mankind must no longer be a fair but empty phrase; it must be given a structure of force and reality. The nations must realize their common life and effect a workable partnership to secure that life against the aggressions of autocratic and self-pleasing power.

For these things we can afford to pour out blood and treasure. For these are the things we have always professed to desire, and unless we pour out blood and treasure now and succeed we may never be able to unite or show conquering force again in the great cause of human liberty. The day has come to conquer or submit. If the forces of autocracy can divide us they will overcome us; if we stand together victory is certain and the liberty which victory will secure. We can afford then to be generous, but we cannot afford then or now to be weak or omit any single guarantee of justice and security.

9

Reply to the Russian Ambassador

As the crisis deepened in Russia, Wilson welcomed the first ambassador of "Free Russia," with a statement that labeled the Bolsheviks as disloyal and (implicitly) in league with foreign intrigue. It was a very short step to the conclusion that the Bolsheviks were German agents.

Document†

Mr. Ambassador, to the keen satisfaction which I derived from the fact that the Government of the United States was the first to welcome, by its official recognition, the new democracy of Russia to the family of free States is added the exceptional pleasure which I experience in now receiving from your hand the letters whereby the provisional Government of Russia accredits you as its ambassador extraordinary and plenipotentiary to the United States and in according to you formal recognition as the first ambassador of free Russia to this country.

For the people of Russia the people of the United States have ever entertained friendly feelings, which have now been greatly deepened by the knowledge that, actuated by the same lofty motives, the two Governments and peoples are coöperating to bring to a successful termination the conflict now raging for human liberty and a universal acknowledgment of those principles of right and justice which should direct all Governments. I feel convinced that when this happy day shall come no small share of the credit will be due to the devoted people of Russia, who, overcoming disloyalty from within and intrigue from without, remain steadfast to the cause.

The mission which it was my pleasure to send to Russia has already assured the provisional Government that in this momentous struggle and in the problems that confront and will confront the free Government of Russia that Government may count on the steadfast friendship of the Government of the United States and its constant coöperation in all desired appropriate directions.

It only remains for me to give expression to my admiration of the way in which the provisional Government of Russia is meeting all requirements, to my entire sympathy with them in their noble object to insure to the people of Russia the blessings of freedom and of equal rights and opportunity, and to my faith that through their efforts Russia will assume her rightful place among the great free nations of the world.

†From: Wilson, "Reply to the Russian Ambassador, Mr. Boris Bahkmeteff, Upon his Presentation of Credentials, "July 5, 1917, Official Bulletin No. 48, in *The Public Papers of Woodrow Wilson*, eds. Dodd and Baker, vol. 5, pp. 71-72.

10

Lenin on Democracy and Revolution

Lenin's discussion of political liberty as only the first object of Marxists, and his belief that the state itself was a product of class antagonisms was at the heart of the Bolshevik-Menshevik split in the first decade of the twentieth century. Both Wilson and Lenin were concerned about concentrations of wealth and power; their remedies led in exactly opposite directions.

Document†

The democratic revolution is a bourgeois revolution. The slogan of Black Redistribution of the land, or "land and liberty"—this most widespread slogan of the peasant masses, downtrodden, and ignorant, yet passionately yearning for light and happiness—is a bourgeois slogan. But we Marxists must know that there is not, nor can there be, any other path to real freedom for the proletariat and the peasantry than the path of bourgeois freedom and bourgeois progress. We must not forget that there is not, nor can there be at the present time, any other means of bringing socialism nearer than by complete political liberty, a democratic republic, a revolutionary- democratic dictatorship of the proletariat and the peasantry. Being the representatives of the advance and of the only revolutionary class, revolutionary without reservations, doubts and retrospection, we must present to the whole of the people the tasks of a democratic revolution as widely and as boldly as possible, and display the maximum of initiative in so doing. . . .

Revolutions are the locomotives of history, said Marx. Revolutions are the festivals of the oppressed and the exploited. At no other time are the masses of the people in a position to come forward so actively as creators of a new social order as at a time of revolution. At such times the people are capable of performing miracles, if judged by a narrow philistine scale of gradual progress. But the leaders of the revolutionary parties must also, at such a time, present their tasks in a wider and bolder fashion, so that their slogan may always be in advance of the revolutionary initiative of the masses, serve them as a beacon and reveal to them our democratic and socialist ideal in all its magnitude and splendour, indicate the shortest, the most direct route to complete, absolute and final victory. . . .

Let the bourgeois opportunists contemplate the future reaction with cowardly fear. The workers will not be frightened either by the thought that

†From: V.I. Lenin, "The Two Tactics of Social-Democracy in The Democratic Revolution," in *V.I. Lenin, Selected Works* (Moscow: Cooperative Publishing Society of Foreign Workers in The USSR, 1933), vol. 3, pp. 121-30.

the reaction proposes to be terrible or by the thought that the bourgeoisie proposes to desert. The workers are not looking forward to striking bargains, they do not ask for sops; they are striving to crush the reactionary forces mercilessly, i.e., to set up a *revolutionary-democratic dictatorship of the proletariat and the peasantry.* . . .

At the head of the whole of the people, and particularly of the peasantry—for complete freedom, for a consistent democratic revolution, for a republic! At the head of all the toilers and the exploited—for socialism! Such must in practice be the policy of the revolutionary proletariat, such is the class slogan which must permeate and determine the solution of every tactical question, and every practical step of the workers' party during the revolution. . . .

Great questions in the life of nations are settled only by force. The reactionary classes are usually themselves the first to resort to violence, to civil war; they are the first to "place the bayonet on the agenda" as Russian autocracy has been doing systematically, consistently, everywhere, all over the country. . . . And since such a situation has arisen, since the bayonet has really taken first place on the political agenda, since the uprising has become necessary and urgent—the constitutional dreams and school exercises in parliamentarism are becoming only a screen for the bourgeois betrayal of the revolution. The genuinely revolutionary class must, then, advance precisely the slogan of dictatorship. . . .

Making corresponding allowances for the concrete national peculiarities and substituting serfdom in place of feudalism, all these propositions will be fully applicable to Russia of 1905. There is no doubt that by learning from the experience of Germany, as elucidated by Marx, we cannot adopt any other slogan for a decisive victory of the revolution than the revolutionary-democratic dictatorship of the proletariat. . . .

The success of the peasant uprising, the victory of the democratic revolution will but clear the way for a genuine and decisive struggle for socialism on the basis of a democratic republic. In this struggle the peasantry as a landowning class will play the same treacherous, vacillating part as that played at present by the bourgeoisie in its struggle for democracy. To forget this means forgetting socialism, deluding oneself and deceiving others with regard to the real interests and tasks of the proletariat. . . .

11

"Maintain Every American Agency in Russia"

In this report to the secretary of state only a few days after the Bolshevik Revolution, Consul General Maddin Summers does not play down the seriousness of the situation but stresses that Americans in Russia could still play a key role by encouraging the better elements. Much debate would take place over the next months on what to do about Russia, but the alternative Wilson chose depended upon similar assumptions and similar mechanisms to carry it out.

Document†

Moscow, *November 17, 1917, 4 p.m.*
[*Received November 20, 2.45 a.m.*]

On the 9th instant Maximalist Party supported by Moscow garrison and workmen armed by Kerensky to fight Kornilov seized government of Moscow. The mayor of city and all authorities supported by officers, students and military cadets, occupied arsenal and strategic points leading to Kremlin. Heavy fighting took place over entire city lasting seven days and accompanied by heavy loss of life and property.

Moscow in chaos, panic may be looked for if the armed workmen begin to loot. All real newspapers stopped and city practically isolated. Maximalists threaten to stop railways to prevent arrival of troops to support Provisional Government.

Americans all safe, many of them going to barracks of french military mission for defense. Consulate and my private residence slightly damaged by rifle and shell fire, houses in immediate vicinity completely demolished.

I cannot too strongly commend Poole's untiring efforts in behalf of Americans in grave danger.

The situation is grave as more serious fighting is expected soon and the Maximalists will not give up the city without great loss of life. Every effort is being made to protect Americans and I may have to draw for considerable sum to meet the emergency and enable them to leave if necessary. I am keeping Embassy advised.

†From: *Foreign Relations of The United States, 1918: Russia*, vol. 1, pp. 234-35.

There is strong feeling amongst the working class against the Allies including America and if the movement is not put down immediately peace may be made with Germany. Even if this be not done Russian troops cannot continue the campaign as they have no food, no discipline and are weary of the war. The difficulties of transport and pressure on the western front will prevent German military advance into heart of Russia this winter but the general disorganization now existing will permit almost unhindered operations by German espionage and propaganda. Our immediate problem is to counteract their work in every way possible. For this purpose as well as to lend moral support to the better elements in Russia, which will regain the upper hand, every effort must be made to maintain every American agency in Russia.

12

"The Dreamers in Russia"

By one of those strange coincidences that dot any historical landscape, Wilson was scheduled to deliver an address to the American Federation of Labor on November 12, 1917. His theme was to be the need for labor to stand together with government and business in the war crisis, but with the Bolshevik Revolution he was now confronted with the need to talk about the activities of a government dedicated to class revolution and peace with America's enemies. His nearly spontaneous reaction to Lenin's appeal for a general armistice was the first indication that he would not chose the alternative of direct dealings with the Bolsheviks.

Document†

May I not say that it is amazing to me that any group of persons should be so ill-informed as to suppose, as some groups in Russia apparently suppose, that any reforms planned in the interest of the people can live in the presence of a Germany powerful enough to undermine or overthrow them by intrigue or force? Any body of free men that compounds with the present German Government is compounding for its own destruction. But that is not the whole of the story. Any man in America or anywhere else that supposes that the free industry and enterprise of the world can continue if the Pan-German plan is achieved and German power fastened upon the world is as fatuous as the dreamers in Russia. What I am opposed to is not the feeling of the pacifists, but their stupidity. My heart is with them, but my mind has a contempt for them. I want peace, but I know how to get it, and they do not.

You will notice that I sent a friend of mine, Colonel House, to Europe, who is as great a lover of peace as any man in the world; but I didn't send him on a peace mission yet. I sent him to take part in a conference as to how the war was to be won, and he knows, as I know, that that is the way to get peace, if you want it for more than a few minutes.

All of this is a preface to the conference that I have referred to with regard to what we are going to do. If we are true friends of freedom, our own or anybody else's, we will see that the power of this country and the productivity of this country are raised to their absolute maximum, and that absolutely nobody is allowed to stand in the way of it. When I say that nobody is allowed to stand in the way I do not mean that he shall be

†From: Wilson, "Address to The American Federation of Labor at Buffalo, NY, November 12, 1917," in *The Public Papers of Woodrow Wilson*, eds. Dodd and Baker, vol. 5, pp. 120-21.

prevented by the power of the Government, but by the power of the American spirit. Our duty, if we are to do this great thing and show America to be what we believe her to be—the greatest hope and energy of the world—is to stand together night and day until the job is finished.

While we are fighting for freedom we must see, among other things, that labor is free; and that means a number of interesting things. It means not only that we must do what we have declared our purpose to do, see that the conditions of labor are not rendered more onerous by the war, but also that we shall see to it that the instrumentalities by which the conditions of labor are improved are not blocked or checked. That we must do. That has been the matter about which I have taken pleasure in conferring from time to time with your president, Mr. Gompers; and if I may be permitted to do so, I want to express my admiration of his patriotic courage, his large vision, and his statesman-like sense of what has to be done. I like to lay my mind alongside of a mind that knows how to pull in harness. The horses that kick over the traces will have to be put in corral.

Now, to stand together means that nobody must interrupt the processes of our energy if the interruption can possibly be avoided without the absolute invasion of freedom. To put it concretely, that means this: nobody has a right to stop the processes of labor until all the methods of conciliation and settlement have been exhausted. And I might as well say right here that I am not talking to you alone. You sometimes stop the courses of labor, but there are others who do the same, and I believe I am speaking from my own experience not only, but from the experience of others when I say that you are reasonable in a larger number of cases than the capitalists. I am not saying these things to them personally yet, because I have not had a chance, but they have to be said, not in any spirit of criticism, but in order to clear the atmosphere and come down to business. Everybody on both sides has now got to transact business, and a settlement is never impossible when both sides want to do the square and right thing.

13

Trotsky on the Secret Treaties

Trotsky's statement upon the release of the secret treaties contained an acknowledgement that the Central Powers could make use of the documents to belittle Allied war aims, but it laid down two challenges: one to the German proletariat to carry out their own revolution and revelation, and one to the Allies to contradict him. Wilson took him up on the second (see Document 17).

Document†

22 November 1917

In publishing the secret diplomatic documents from the foreign policy archives of Tsarism and of the bourgeois coalition Governments of the first seven months of the revolution, we are carrying out the undertaking which we made when our party was in opposition. Secret diplomacy is a necessary tool for a propertied minority which is compelled to deceive the majority in order to usbject it to its interests. Imperialism, with its dark plans of conquest and its robber alliances and deals, developed the system of secret diplomacy to the highest level. The struggle against the imperialism which is exhausting and destroying the peoples of Europe is at the same time a struggle against capitalist diplomacy, which has cause enough to fear the light of day. The Russian people, and the peoples of Europe and the whole world, should learn the documentary truth about the plans forged in secret by the financiers and industrialists together with their parliamentary and diplomatic agents. The peoples of Europe have paid for the right to this truth with countless sacrifices and universal economic desolation.

The abolition of secret diplomacy is the primary condition for an honest, popular, truly democratic foreign policy. The Soviet Government regards it as its duty to carry out such a policy in practice. That is precisely why, while openly proposing an immediate armistice to all the belligerent peoples and their Governments, we are at the same time publishing these treaties and agreements, which have lost all binding force for the Russian workers, soldiers, and peasants who have taken power into their own hands.

†From: Jane Degras, ed., *Soviet Documents on Foreign Policy* (London: Oxford University Press, 1951), vol. 1, pp. 7-8.

The bourgeois politicians and journalists of Germany and Austria-Hungary may try to make use of the documents published in order to present the diplomacy of the Central Empires in a more advantageous light. But any such attempt would be doomed to pitiful failure, and that for two reasons. In the first place, we intend quickly to place before the tribunal of public opinion secret documents which treat sufficiently clearly of the diplomacy of the Central Empires. Secondly, and more important, the methods of secret diplomacy are as universal as imperialist robbery. When the German proletariat enters the revolutionary path leading to the secrets of their chancelleries, they will extract documents no whit inferior to those which we are about to publish. It only remains to hope that this will take place quickly.

The workers' and peasants' Government abolishes secret diplomacy and its intrigues, codes, and lies. We have nothing to hide. Out programme expresses the ardent wishes of millions of workers, soldiers, and peasants. We want peace as soon as possible on the basis of decent coexistence and collaboration of the peoples. We want the rule of capital to be overthrown as soon as possible. In exposing to the entire world the work of the ruling classes, as expressed in the secret diplomatic documents, we address the workers with the the call which forms the unchangeable foundation of our foreign policy: 'Proletarians of all countries, unite.'

14

Russia's "Peace Initiative"

The dual nature of Soviet foreign policy, which had to cover the interests of revolution in Russia as well as the world revolution, led to many repetitions of this early statement to the West. Trotsky obviously wanted recognition and legitimacy, and was hinting he would deal with either Allied governments or their peoples to get it. It was up to the capitalists to choose. Awareness of just these sorts of complications helped to produce the confused reaction to Lenin's government outside Russia.

Document†

Petrograd, *November 27, 1917, 10 p.m.*
Received November 30, 12.20 p.m.]

Chiefs of Allied military missions and military attachés were called to the General Staff 3 p.m. to-day and given following communication in French and Russian from Trotsky. Reply from military attachés was that communication would be handed to their respective Ambassadors. Following translation made by Military Mission:

1. As evidenced by all our steps, we are striving for general and not separate armistice. To a separate armistice we may be forced by our allies if they will close their eyes before the facts.

2. We are ready at any moment with any representatives of the Allies (translator thinks this means any of the Allies) to conduct negotiations for immediate accomplishment of an armistice.

We did not demand a parliamentary "recognition." We are recognized by the people.

We want business negotiations. We reserve the right to publish protocols for the information of all.

3. That negative attitude with which our peace initiative is being met from the side of several of the Allied Governments, cannot in the slightest change the course of our policy.

The Allies should answer: are they willing to begin negotiations for immediate armistice aiming at the conclusion of peace and democartic principles? Are they agreeable to support our initiative in this direction? Do they demand other measures? What kind?

As long as Allied Governments answer with bare "no recognition" of us and our initiative we will follow our own course appealing to the peoples

†From: *Foreign Relations of the United States, 1918: Russia*, vol. 1, p. 250.

after the governments. Should the results of the appeal bring separate peace, which we do not want, responsibility will fall completely upon the Allied Governments. Trotsky.

15

Trotsky on International Relations

Trotsky's sweeping review of the international situation before the Central Executive Committee of the party dwelt on differences between the capitalist powers. Perhaps his private review of the exchanges with Ambassador Francis in 1916 (see Document 5) suggested to him that America was panting to get into Russia, and would therefore oppose intervention if it could be assured of economic opportunities. To that extent, at least, America was supposed to be different from a country like Great Britain which had a big stake in the restoration of the old order. Trotsky's interpretation of Wilson's decision to go to war, on the other hand, did not speak well of his grasp on reality. But there is a recognition here that *both* Lenin and Wilson are talking about a new order.

Document†

21 November 1917

Our policy in the field of international relations is dictated by the decree on peace adopted by the All-Russian Congress of Soviets. The very fact of its adoption was unexpected for the old routine habits of thought of the European bourgeois world, and the decree was first taken as a party declaration rather than as a definite act of State power. It was not until the lapse of some time that the ruling classes of Europe began to realize that they were dealing with a proposal emanating from a State which represented many millions of people. The bourgeoisie of the Allied countries adopted an extremely hostile attitude towards this decree. The attitude of the Governments of the enemy countries was ambiguous, and could not have been otherwise. On the one hand, the revolution interested them as a means of aggravating the confusion in Russia and of improving their own military prospects, and this was a cause for rejoicing. On the other hand, in so far as they understood that they were dealing not with an ephemeral phenomenon, capable only of disorganizing, in so far as they saw that the Soviet Government was supported by the large armed masses, to that extent they could not fail to recognize that the victory of the Soviets was a fact of the greatest international importance. In this respect the attitude in Germany towards the news of the victory over Kerensky is significant. Our broadcast from Tsarskoe Selo was picked up by the Austrians, but the Hamburg radio tried to jam the broadcast of the telegram. The ambiguity in the German

†From: Degras, ed., *Soviet Documents*, vol. 1, pp. 4-7.

attitude consists in the fact that as Germans they are ready to rejoice; as bourgeois propertied classes they see that they have cause to fear.

The Soviet Government had to formulate proposals for peace negotiations and an armistice. Military and political circumstances have, up to now, not been favourable to the completion of this political step. Krasnov's detachment was at the approaches to Petersburg, and it had to be assumed that it would be followed by other units. In Moscow we still struggled for power. The news from the provinces was indefinite, partly because of the so-called neutrality of the postal and telegraph union.

In western Europe the mood was one of waiting. There was lack of confidence in the new Soviet Government. The mass of the workers had confidence in the Government, but there was fear that it would not be able to survive. Now the Government has been established as a reality in both capitals of the country, in many important provincial centres, among the vast majority of the army, and it is attracting the peasant masses. These facts are indisputable. . . .

Now even the most hardened European diplomats appreciate that it is impossible to smash the Soviet Government either in a day, or in a week. They are confronted with the complete political helplessness of the bourgeoisie in Russia, in spite of its enormous economic power. They have to reckon with the Soviet Government as a fact, and to establish certain relations with it. These relations are being formed empirically, in practice; the agents of the European Powers are compelled to approach us with all sorts of questions concerning current matters, such as questions of leaving or entering the country, etc. With regard to political relations, this is not uniform on the part of the various Powers. Probably the most hostile of them is the Government of Great Britain, the country whose upper bourgeoisie risk losing less than anybody else from the war, and hope to gain most. The drawn-out nature of the war is not in the least inconsistent with British policy. As to France, the majority of the petty-bourgeois democracy are peacefully inclined, but they are helpless. The petty-bourgeois Cabinet is dependent on the Stock Exchange. The small French shopkeeper is a pacifist and does not personally know anything about those secret treaties and imperialist aims for which he sheds his blood. France had suffered most from the war. France feels that the prolongation of the war threatens it with degeneration and death. The struggle of the working class against war is growing. The acuteness of the situation in France and the growth of the opposition on the part of the working class within the country has led to France reacting to the creation of Soviet power by forming the Clemenceau Ministry. Clemenceau is a radical of the extreme jacobin chauvinist wing. In the course of three years of war he could not form his own Ministry; the Clemenceau Ministry now formed without the participation of the socialists and directed against the socialists is a convulsion of the French petty-bourgeois democracy, terror-stricken by the setting up of the Soviet Government. Petty-bourgeois France considers us to be a Government in alliance with Wilhelm, and perhaps a Government of struggle against France.

The scanty news from Italy speaks about the enthusiasm with which the working class greeted the Soviet Government. Italy hesitated for nine months which camp it would be more advantageous to join, and in the course of those nine months the working class of Italy had an opportunity of recognizing the fatal effect of collaboration of the proletariat with the bourgeoisie. As to the middle classes and the peasantry, they became disillusioned in this war, and this disillusionment provided a favourable sounding-board for the protesting voice of the proletariat.

The United States began to intervene in the war after three years, under the influence of the sober calculations of the American Stock Exchange. America could not tolerate the victory of one coalition over the other. America is interested in the weakening of both coalitions and in the consolidation of the hegemony of American capital. Apart from that, American war. During the war American exports have more than doubled and have reached a figure not reached by any other capitalist State. Exports go almost entirely to the Allied countries. When in January Germany came out for unrestricted U-boat warfare, all railway stations and harbours in the United States were overloaded with the output of the war industries. Transport was disorganized and New York witnessed food riots such as we ourselves have never seen here. Then the finance capitalists sent an ultimatum to Wilson: to secure the sale of the output of the war industries within the country. Wilson accepted the ultimatum, and hence the preparations for war and war itself. America does not aim at territorial conquests; America can be tolerant with regard to the existence of the Soviet Government, since it is satisfied with the exhaustion of the Allied countries and Germany. Apart from that America is interested in investing its capital in Russia.

As to Germany, its internal economic situation forces it to take up an attitude of semi-tolerance towards the Soviet Government. The peace proposals made by Germany are partly feelers: partly they were dictated by the anxiety to lay responsibility for the continuation of the war on the other side.

All of the news we have about the impression made in Europe by the decree on peace proves that our most optimistic assumptions were justified. The German working class is fully aware of what is happening in Russia at present; perhaps it appreciates these events even better than people in Russia itself. The actions of the working class in Russia are more revolutionary than their consciousness; but the consciousness of the European working class has developed over decades; and, starting from a class analysis of the events now taking place in Russia, the proletariat of the West understands that power has not been seized here by a handful of conspirators with the support of the Red Guard and the sailors, as the bourgeois press tries to make out; it understands that here a new epoch in the history of the world is beginning. The working class have taken the machinery of state into their own hands, and this machinery must necessarily become the instrument of the struggle for peace. A fatal blow was dealt to war on the historic night of 25 October [7 November]. War as a colossal enterprise of the various classes and groups is dead. The European Governments are no longer concerned with the realization of their initial aims, but with the liquidation of this enterprise with the least possible damage to their rule. It is not possible for either side to think of victory; and the intervention of the working class in this conflict is a factor of immeasurable importance. The decree on peace is being widely broadcast throughout Europe. The war is at its last gasp and it is the task of the Soviet Government to deal it a final blow by the formal proposal of peace negotiations.

16

"Nothing is to be Gained from Inaction"

Secretary Lansing's first serious proposal for intervention in the Russia situation was posited on the premise that there was nothing to be hoped for from Bolshevik domination. It had taken Lansing just one month to arrive at that conclusion; no serious exploration of Bolshevik attitudes been undertaken. Since it did not involve direct American military aid, perhaps the secretary of state reasoned that by not letting Kaledin and the Cossacks know of American attitudes the United States was also intervening on behalf of the Bolsheviks. The United States had chosen a very similar watchful waiting alternative in Mexico.

Document†

Washington, *December 10, 1917.*

My Dear Mr. President: I have been considering the Russian situation and, although our information is meager and to an extent confusing, I have reached the following conclusions:

That the Bolsheviki are determined to prevent Russia from taking further part in the war.

That the longer they continue in power the more will authority in Russia be disorganized and the more will the armies disintegrate, and the harder it will become to restore order and military efficiency.

That the elimination of Russia as a fighting force will prolong the war for two or three years, with a corresponding demand upon this country for men and money.

That with Bolsheviki domination broken the Russian armies might be reorganized and become an important factor in the war by next spring or summer.

That the hope of a stable Russian Government lies for the present in a military dictatorship backed by loyal disciplined troops.

That the only apparent nucleus for an organized movement sufficiently strong to supplant the Bolsheviki and establish a government would seem to be the group of general officers with General Kaledin, the hetman of the Don Cossacks.

These conclusions present the problem as to whether we ought to take any steps to encourage the Kaledin party, and if so the nature of those steps.

†From: *Foreign Relations: The Lansing Papers, 1914-1920*, vol. 2, pp. 343-45.

I think that we must assume that Kaledin and his Cossacks know less about us and our attitude than we know about them, that through Bolshevik and German sources they are being furnished with false information and very probably have been told that we have recognized the Bolshevik Government and so are coming to the conclusion that further resistance is useless. Of course to have this group broken up would be to throw the country into the hands of the Bolsheviki and the Germans could freely continue their propaganda which is leading to chaos and the actual disintegration of the Russian Empire.

A possible way of checking this is to get a message through to Kaledin (probably via Tiflis and courier) telling the true state of affairs, and non-recognition of the Bolsheviki and our readiness to give recognition to a government which exhibits strength enough to restore order and a purpose to carry out in good faith Russia's international engagements.

Whether such a communication is advisable is, I think, worthy of consideration, but if it is to be sent it ought to be done without delay as I am convinced that German intrigues and Bolshevik false representations will speedily impair the morale of Kaledin's followers unless something is done to give them hope that they will, if their movement gains sufficient strength, receive moral and material aid from this Government. It seems to me that nothing is to be gained by inaction, that it is simply playing into the Bolsheviki's hands, and that the situation may be saved by a few words of encouragement, and the saving of Russia means the saving to this country of hundreds of thousands of men and billions of collars. I do not see how we could be any worse off if we took this course because we have absolutely nothing to hope from continued Bolshevik domination.

In regard to Kaledin and the Russian generals, Alexieff, Brousiloff and Korniloff, who appear to be with him or about to join him, I have inquired of Major Washburne, who knew them personally and more or less intimately. From him I gained the following:

Kaledin is a man of ponderous determination, who is unaffected alike by victory or defeat. He is a strong character who carried through his purposes regardless of opposition. As a commander he resembles Grant. He radiates force and mastery.

Alexieff is a modest, quiet man, but the most skillfull strategist in Russia, if not in any of the allied countries. He listens patiently, talks little and reaches his decisions alone.

Brousiloff is the most brilliant general in the Russian armies and arouses the enthusiasm of the soldiers and his subordinates by his ability and forceful personality. As a strategist he is only second to Alexieff. While Kaledin is a man of the people. Brousiloff is of the aristocracy.

Korniloff is not the equal of any one of the three other generals in military skill or in personal popularity with the troops. He has, however, considerable influence with soldiers recruited in Siberia and Turkestan.

The foregoing indicates the elements of strength in the military group which seem to be gathering about Kaledin, and which will in all probability obtain the support of the Cadets and of all the *bourgeoisie* and the land-owning class.

I would like to talk this matter over with you after Cabinet meeting tomorrow if that meets your convenience.

Faithfully yours,
Robert Lansing

Decision in Principle

Wilson and Lansing obviously did not believe that Lenin represented the will of the Russian people. There was no question that Lenin did not control the territory of Russia in December, 1917, but however one viewed this decision it amounted to interference in the internal politics of a friendly country, for whatever reason it was undertaken.

Document†

Washington, *December 12, 1917.*

My Dear Mr. President: After consultation with Secretary McAdoo today, and in line with our talk last evening, I have prepare the enclosed telegram which Secretary McAdoo approves.

If it meets with your approval will you be good enough to send it to the telegraph office of the Department so that it can immediately be put upon the wires? [Wilson sent his approval on the same day.]

Faithfully yours,
Robert Lansing

[Enclosure]

Draft Telegram to the Ambassador in Great Britain (Page)

For Crosby [Assistant Secretary of the Threasury.] The Russian situation has been carefully considered and the conclusion has been reached that the movement in the south and southeast under the leadership of Kaledine and Korniloff offers at the present time the greatest hope for the reestablishment of a stable government and the continuance of a military force on the German and Austrian fronts. While there can be no certainty of the success of Kaledine it is not improbable that he may succeed. From Moscow and Tiflis come very favorable reports as to the strength of the movement and as to the weakening power of the Bolsheviki.

In view of the policy being pursued by Lenine and Trotsky which if continued will remove Russia as a factor in the war and may even make her resources available to the Central Powers, any movement tending to prevent such a calamity should be encouraged even though its success is only a possibility.

†From: *Foreign Relations: The Lansing Papers, 1914-1920,* vol. 2, p. 345.

18

The Fourteen Points

As well known as it is to historians and students, Wilson's Fourteen Points speech is almost always regarded as having to do with a general peace program, and seldom put in the context of Russian-American competition for the minds of men. Yet almost every point was designed to meet head-on the claims Trotsky made when he released the secret treaties. It was also designed to take into account the general desire for peace stimulated by the Russian Revolution by giving "all the governments and peoples associated together against the Imperialists" [a carefully chosen world] something to fight for, and something with which to resist the blandishments of Lenin's appeal to the working classes of the world.

Document†

Once more, as repeatedly before, the spokesmen of the Central Empires have indicated their desire to discuss the objects of the war and the possible bases of a general peace. Parleys have been in progress at Brest-Litovsk between representatives of the Central Powers to which the attention of all the belligerents has been invited for the purpose of ascertaining whether it may be possible to extend these parleys into a general conference with regard to terms of peace and settlement. The Russian representatives presented not only a perfectly definite statement of the principles upon which they would be willing to conclude peace but also an equally definite program of the concrete application of those principles. The representatives of the Central Powers, on their part, presented an outline of settlement which, if much less definite, seemed susceptible of liberal interpretation until their specific program of practical terms was added. That program proposed no concessions at all either to the sovereignty of Russia or to the preferences of the populations with whose fortunes it dealt, but meant, in a word, that the Central Empires were to keep every foot of territory their armed forces had occupied,—every province, every city, every point of vantage,—as a permanent addition to their territories and their power. It is a reasonable conjecture that the general principles of settlement which they at first suggested originated with the more liberal statesmen of Germany and Austria, the men who have begun to feel the force of their own peoples' thought and purpose, while the concrete terms of actual settlement came from the military leaders who have no thought but to keep what they have got. The negotiations have been

†From: Wilson, "Address Delivered at a Joint Session of the two Houses of Congress," January 8, 1918, in *The Public Papers of Woodrow Wilson*, eds. Dodd and Baker, vol. 5, pp. 155-62.

broken off. The Russian representatives were sincere and in earnest. They cannot entertain such proposals of conquest and domination.

The whole incident is full of significance. It is also full of perplexity. With whom are the Russian representatives dealing? For whom are the representatives of the Central Empires speaking? Are they speaking for the majorities of their respective parliaments or for the minority parties, that military and imperialistic minority which has so far dominated their whole policy and controlled the affairs of Turkey and of the Balkan states which have felt obliged to become their associates in this war? The Russian representatives have insisted, very justly, very wisely, and in the true spirit of modern democracy, that the conferences they have been holding with the Teutonic and Turkish statesmen should be held within open, not closed, doors, and all the world has been audience, as was desired. To whom have we been listening, then? To those who speak the spirit and intention of the Resolutions of the German Reichstag of the ninth of July last, the spirit and intention of the liberal leaders and parties of Germany, or to those who resist and defy that spirit and intention and insist upon conquest and subjugation? or are we listening, in fact, to both, unreconciled and in open and hopeless contradiction? These are very serious and pregnant questions. Upon the answer to them depends the peace of the world.

But, whatever the results of the parleys at Brest-Litovsk, whatever the confusions of counsel and of purpose in the utterances of the spokesmen of the Central Empires, they have again attempted to acquaint the world with their objects in the war and have again challenged their adversaries to say what their objects are and what sort of settlement they would deem just and satisfactory. There is no good reason why that challenge should not be responded to, and responded to with the utmost candor. We did not wait for it. Not once, but again and again, we have laid our whole thought and purpose before the world, not in general terms only, but each time with sufficient definition to make it clear what sort of definitive terms of settlement must necessarily spring out of them. Within the last week Mr. Lloyd George has spoken with admirable candor and in admirable spirit for the people and Government of Great Britain. There is no confusion of counsel among the adversaries of the Central powers, no uncertainty of principle, no vagueness of detail. The only secrecy of counsel, the only lack of fearless frankness, the only failure to make definite statement of the objects of the war, lies with Germany and her Allies. The issues of life and death hang upon these definitions. No statesman who has the least conception of his responsibility ought for a moment to permit himself to continue this tragical and appalling outpouring of blood and treasure unless he is sure beyond a peradventure that the objects of the vital sacrifice are part and parcel of the very life of Society and that the people for whom he speaks think them right and imperative as he does.

There is, moreover, a voice calling for these definitions of principle and of purpose which is, it seems to me, more thrilling and more compelling than any of the many moving voices with which the troubled air of the world is filled. It is the voice of the Russian people. They are prostrate and all but helpless, it would seem, before the grim power of Germany, which has hitherto known no relenting and no pity. Their power, apparently, is shattered. And yet their soul is not subservient. They will not yield either in principle or in action. Their conception of what is right, of what it is humane and honorable for them to accept, has been stated with a frankness, a largeness of view, a generosity of spirit, and a universal human sympathy which must challenge the admiration of every friend of mankind; and they have refused to compound their ideals or desert others that they themselves may be safe. They call to us to say what it is that we desire, in what, if in anything, our purpose and our spirit differ from theirs; and I believe that the people of the United States would wish me to respond, with utter simplicity and frankness. Whether their present leaders believe it or not, it is our heartfelt desire and hope that some way may be opened whereby we may be privileged to assist the people of Russia to attain their utmost hope of liberty and ordered peace.

It will be our wish and purpose that the processes of peace, when they are begun, shall be absolutely open and that they shall involve and permit henceforth no secret understandings of any kind. The day of conquest and aggrandizement is gone by; so is also the day of secret covenants entered into in the interest of particular governments and likely at some unlooked-for moment to upset the peace of the world. It is this happy fact, now clear to the view of every public man whose thoughts do not still linger in an age that is dead and gone, which makes it possible for every nation whose purposes are consistent with justice and the peace of the world to avow now or at any other time the objects it has in view.

We entered this war because violations of right had occurred which touched us to the quick and made the life of our own people impossible unless they were corrected and the world secured once for all against their recurrence. What we demand in this war, therefore, is nothing peculiar to ourselves. It is that the world be made fit and safe to live in; and particularly that it be made safe for every peace-loving nation which, like our own, wishes to live its own life, determine its own institutions, be assured of justice and fair dealing by the other peoples of the world as against force and selfish aggression. All the peoples of the world are in effect partners in this interest, and for our own part we see very clearly that unless justice be done to others it will not be done to us. The program of the world's peace, therefore, is our program; and that program, the only possible program, as we see it, is this:

I. Open covenants of peace, openly arrived at, after which there shall be no private international understanding of any kind but diplomacy shall proceed always frankly and in the public view.

II. Absolute freedom of navigation upon the seas, outside territorial waters, alike in peace and in war, except as the seas may be closed in whole or in part by international action for the enforcement of international covenants.

III. The removal, so far as possible, of all economic barriers and the establishment of an equality of trade conditions among all the nations consenting to the peace and associating themselves for its maintenance.

IV. Adequate guarantees given and taken that national armaments will be reduced to the lowest point consistent with domestic safety.

V. A free, open-minded, and absolutely impartial adjustment of all colonial claims, based upon a strict observance of the principle that in determining all such questions of sovereignty the interests of the populations concerned must have equal weight with the equitable claims of the government whose title is to be determined.

VI. The evacuation of all Russian territory and such a settlement of all questions affecting Russia as will secure the best and freest coöperation of the other nations of the world in obtaining for her an unhampered and unembarrassed opportunity for the independent determination of her own political development and national policy and assure her of a sincere welcome into the society of free nations under institutions of her own choosing; and, more than a welcome, assistance also of every kind that she may need and may herself desire. The treatment accorded Russia by her sister nations in the months to come will be the acid test of their good will, of their comprehension of her needs as distinguished from their own interests, and of their intelligent and unselfish sympathy.

VII. Belgium, the whole world will agree, must be evacuated and restored, without any attempt to limit the sovereignty which she enjoys in common with all other free nations. No other single act will serve as this will serve to restore confidence among the nations in the laws which they have themselves set and determined for the government of their relations with one another. Without this healing act the whole structure and validity of international law is forever impaired.

VIII. All French territory should be freed and the invaded portions restored, and the wrong done to France by Prussia in 1871 in the matter of Alsace-Lorraine, which has unsettled the peace of the world for nearly fifty years, should be righted, in order that peace may once more be made secure in the interest of all.

IX. A readjustment of the frontiers of Italy should be effected along clearly recognizable lines of nationality.

X. The peoples of Austria-Hungary, whose place among the nations we wish to see safeguarded and assured, should be accorded the freest opportunity of autonomous development.

XI. Rumania, Serbia, and Montenegro should be evacuated; occupied territories restored; Serbia accorded free and secure access to the sea; and the relations of the several Balkan states to one another determined by friendly counsel along historically established lines of allegiance and nationality; and international guarantees of the political and economic independence and territorial integrity of the several Balkan states should be entered into.

XII. The Turkish portions of the present Ottoman Empire should be assured a secure sovereignty, but the other nationalities which are now under

Turkish rule should be assured an undoubted security of life and an absolutely unmolested opportunity of autonomous development, and the Dardanelles should be permanently opened as a free passage to the ships and commerce of all nations under international guarantees.

XIII. An independent Polish state should be erected which should include the territories inhabited by indisputably Polish populations, which should be assured a free and secure access to the sea, and whose political and economic independence and territorial integrity should be guaranteed by international covenant.

XIV. A general association of nations must be formed under specific covenants for the purpose of affording mutual guarantees of political independence and territorial integrity to great and small states alike.

In regard to these essential rectifications of wrong and assertions of right we feel ourselves to be intimate partners of all the governments and peoples associated together against the Imperialists. We cannot be separated in interest or divided in purpose. We stand together until the end.

For such arrangements and covenants we are willing to fight and to continue to fight until they are achieved; but only because we wish the right to prevail and desire a just and stable peace such as can be secured only by removing the chief provocations to war, which this program does remove. We have no jealousy of German greatness, and there is nothing in this program that impairs. it. We grudge her no achievement or distinction of learning or of pacific enterprise such as have made her record very bright and very enviable. We do not wish to injure her or to block in any way her legitimate influence or power. We do not wish to fight her either with arms or with hostile arrangements of trade if she is willing to associate herself with us and the other peace-loving nations of the world in covenants of justice and law and fair dealing. We wish her only to accept a place of equality among the peoples of the world,—the new world in which we now live,—instead of a place of mastery.

Neither do we presume to suggest to her any alteration or modification of her institutions. But it is necessary, we must frankly say, and necessary as a preliminary to any intelligent dealings with her on our part, that we should know whom her spokesmen speak for when they speak to us, whether for the Reichstag majority or for the military party and the men whose creed is imperial domination.

We have spoken now, surely, in terms too concrete to admit of any further doubt or question. An evident principle runs through the whole program I have outlined. It is the principle of justice to all peoples and nationalities, and their right to live on equal terms of liberty and safety with one another, whether they be strong or weak. Unless this principle be made its foundation no part of the structure of international justice can stand. The people of the United States could act upon no other principle; and to the vindication of this principle they are ready to devote their lives, their honor, and everything that they possess. The moral climax of this the culminating and final war for human liberty has come, and they are ready to put their own strength, their own highest purpose, their own integrity and devotion to the test.

19

Trotsky's Questions for America

Trotsky's "what if" inquiry of Raymond Robins had strong overtones of a ploy to divide the Allies and thus delay or prevent an intervention. Even so, if there was ever a time for Wilson to move toward establishing formal relations (*Alternative 1*) Trotsky's gambit offered such an opportunity. He could not answer such a note directly, however, without seeming to accept the contentions of the Bolsheviks that the Japanese and the British were conniving for the destruction of their government. This was perhaps not an unmanageable problem for someone of Wilson's ingenuity, had he been inclined to solve it.

Document†

5 March 1918

In case (*a*) the all-Russian congress of the Soviets will refuse to ratify the peace treaty with Germany, or (*b*) if the German government, breaking the peace treaty, will renew the offensive in order to continue its robbers' raid, or (*c*) if the Soviet government will be forced by the actions of Germany to renounce the peace treaty—before or after its ratification—and to renwe hostilities—

In all these cases, it is very important for the military and political plans of the Soviet power for replies to be given to the following questions:

1. Can the Soviet government rely on the support of the United States of North America, Great Britain, and France in its struggle against Germany?
2. What kind of support could be furnished in the nearest future, and on what conditions—military equipment, transportation supplies, living necessities?
3. What kind of support would be furnished particularly and especially by the United States?

Should Japan—in consequence of an open or tacit understanding with Germany or without such an understanding—attempt to seize Vladivostok and the Eastern-Siberian Railway, which would threaten to cut off Russia from the Pacific Ocean and would greatly impede the concentration of Soviet troops toward the East about the Urals—in such case what steps would be taken by the other allies, particularly and especially by the United States, to

†From: Degras, ed., *Soviet Document*, vol. 1, pp. 56-57.

prevent a Japanese landing on our Far East and to insure uninterrupted communications with Russia through the Siberian route?

In the opinion of the Government of the United States, to what extent—under the above-mentioned circumstances—would aid be assured from Great Britain through Murmansk and Archangel? What steps could the Government of Great Britain undertake in order to assure this aid and thereby to undermine the foundation of the rumors of the hostile plans against Russia on the part of Great Britain in the nearest future?

All these questions are conditioned with the self-understood assumption that the internal and foreign policies of the Soviet government will continue to be directed in accord with the principles of international socialism and that the Soviet government retains its complete independence of all non-socialist governments.

20

Wilson's Reply

Wilson's indirect response to Trotsky's specific inquiries was sufficient to indicate to the Bolsheviks where the president stood, yet ambiguous enough to seem responsive to "liberals" who expected a great deal from Wilson.

Document†

May I not take advantage of the meeting of the Congress of the Soviets to express the sincere sympathy which the people of the United States feel for the Russian people at this moment when the German power has been thrust in to interrupt and turn back the whole struggle for freedom and substitute the wishes of Germany for the purposes of the people of Russia?

Although the Government of the United States is unhappily not now in a position to render the direct and effective aid it would wish to render, I beg to assure the people of Russia through the Congress that it will avail itself of every opportunity to secure for Russia once more complete sovereignty and independence in her own affairs and full restoration to her great role in the life of Europe and the modern world.

The whole heart of the people of the United States is with the people of Russia in the attempt to free themselves forever from autocratic government and become the masters of their own life.

†From: "Message to the People of Russia through the Soviet Congress," March 11, 1918, Official Bulletin, No. 255, in, *The Public Papers of Woodrow Wilson,* vol. 5, p. 191.

21

Japanese Intervention in Siberia

If the United States was not in a position to aid the Russian people, said the Allies, Japan was and ought to be given a chance to straighten things out in Siberia. Wilson came up with a formula which he hoped would satisfy Japan yet reassert American freedom of action. The notion that he was saving Siberia from a German invasion, as he well knew, was preposterous on the face of it. For that reason alone Wilson was wise to withdraw this message.

Document†

Draft Telegram to the Ambassador in Japan (Morris)

The Government of the United States is made constantly aware at every turn of events that it is the desire of the people of the United States that, while cooperating with all its energy with its associates in the war in every direct enterprise of the war in which it is possible for it to take part, it should leave itself diplomatically free wherever it can do so without injustice to its associates. It is for this reason that the Government of the United States has not thought it wise to join the governments of the Entente in asking the Japanese government to act in Siberia. It has no objection to that request being made, and it wishes to assure the Japanese government that it has entire confidence that in putting an armed force into Siberia it is doing so as an ally of Russia, with no purpose but to save Siberia from the invasion of the armies and intrigues of Germany and with entire willingness to leave the determination of all questions that may affect the permanent fortunes of Siberia to the Council of Peace.

†From: Wilson to Morris, March 1, 1918, in *Foreign Relations: The Lansing Papers, 1914-1920*, vol. 2, p. 355.

22

Counterarguments to Intervention

Breckinridge Long's memorandum sets out the arguments which led to Wilson's reconsideration of his decision not to stand in the way of a unilateral Japanese intervention in Siberia. It also suggests another alternative more in line with Wilsonian thinking on world problems. Note also that there is no discussion of a serious German military threat to Siberia; instead Long speaks of commercial intrigue and propaganda, a near-synonym for Bolshevism.

Document†

March 3, 1918.

Mr. Sookine, formerly Secretary at the Russian Embassy, called this afternoon. He said that he had come at the urgent request of his Ambassador who would not come himself because he had gone to New York to lay the same matter before Colonel House.

He opposed the sole intervention by Japan in Siberia on the grounds—
(1) That it would alienate the people of Siberia and Russia in general, and the population of the districts which were occupied by Japanese in particular, from the Allied cause;
(2) That the distrust which the people of Russia felt for Japan was greater than the antipathy which they had towards Germany.

He stated that it would facilitate the German economic and political control of Russia—
(a) By inducing the people to accept German organization and control rather than Japanese;
(b) By offering an argument for Germany to use against the Allied cause and Japan by holding up the specter of Japanese control of Siberia and, possibly, Russia.

He advocated a military political expedition into Russia to be composed of two Japanese armed corps and such fragmentary military units as the United States, France and England could send, even if the British contingent was composed of Indian troops and the French contingent composed of such soldiers as may now be in Cochin China. He advocated a political head of this expedition to be a committee of the Allies, or an American diplomatic representative, especially designated, which, or who, would be in control of the expedition.

†From: *Foreign Relations, 1918: Russia*, vol. 2, pp. 61-63.

He argued that, while the better element of the Russian people were still opposed to Germany, he feared that Germany would diplomatically proceed in her entrance into Russia by restoring order and by bringing about organization, upon which she would predicate the argument that she desired peace, that she wanted cooperation with Russia, that she desired peaceful economic and industrial intercourse and development and could say that the only objection and obstacle to peace was the ambition of the military powers opposing Germany on the western front. He said that he feared that the Russian people might be seduced into accepting the situation and that he believed, from his interpretation of Hertling's most recent speech, that that would be the German policy.

He argued that Germany's policy in Russia would be not only military but a diplomatic endeavor to influence and control the social, economic and industrial elements of the country. He argued that the way to offset and counteract the success of this movement would be to establish a political base as close to the eastern side of the Ural Mountains as possible and to conduct from such a base, supported by the military expedition, a campaign against the German campaign of diplomacy and propaganda.

He realized the physical difficulties preventing any military cooperation on the part of the United States and fully realized the danger consequent to the arming, releasing and organizing of the German and Austrian prisoners near Irkutsk and in Trans-Baikal, particularly with regard to destroying the railroad, or sections of the railroad, or bridges. There is one bridge right near the border of Manchuria which is one of the longest and highest bridges in the world and which, if destroyed, would break completely the line of communication and which it would take two years to rebuild.

The impression which I received from him was that he and Mr. Bakhmeteff feared the intervention of Japan as the mandatory of the Allies but were slowly coming to realize the imminence and the necessity for that particular kind of intervention but that they were endeavoring to do everything in their power to subordinate Japan to the actual supervision and control of the Allies while Japan should be in Siberia. Irrespective of this interpretation, there is considerable force to his argument and a great deal of merit in the suggestion that a political base be established in western Siberia or in eastern Russia to combat, as far as possible, the diplomatic and commercial intrigues and the propaganda of Germany. Of course, this political base would have to be supported by a large military force, much greater than two army corps, which should stretch along, protect, guard and hold the only line of communications to the eastward, which is the Trans-Siberian Railroad.

BRECKINRIDGE LONG

23

Rejection of Japanese Intervention

Wilson's second draft was a complete rejection of Japanese military action in Siberia. The complicated diplomacy with the Allies at this time (see Documents 19 and 20) helps to explain the difficulty Wilson had with Trotksy's questions, but by refusing to go along with a Japanese intervention[the president made things difficult for himself with both the Allies and the Bolsheviks. He was, as he later wrote House, beginning to sweat blood over the Russian problem.

Document†

The Acting Secretary of State to the Ambassador in Japan (Morris)

[Telegram]

Washignton, *March 5, 1918, 4 p.m.*

At your earliest opportunity you will please read to the Japanese Government the following message but leave no copy unless they request you to do so:

The Government of the United states has been giving the most careful and anxious consideration to the conditions now prevailing in Siberia and their possible remedy. It realizes the extreme danger of anarchy to which the Siberian provinces are exposed and the imminent risk also of German invasion and domination. It shares with the governments of the Entente the view that, if intervention is deemed wise, the Government of Japan is in the best situation to undertake it and could accomplish it most efficiently. It has, moreover, the utmost confidence in the Japanese Government and would be entirely willing, so far as its own feelings towards that Government are concerned, to intrust the enterprise to it. But it is bound in frankness to say that the wisdom of intervention seems to it most questionable. If it were undertaken the Government of the United States assumes that the most explicit assurances would be given that it was undertaken by Japan as an ally of Russia, in Russia's interest, and with the sole view of holding it safe against Germany and at the absolute disposal of the final peace conference. Otherwise the Central powers could and would make it appear that Japan was doing in the East exactly what Germany is doing in the West and so seek to counter the condemnation which all the world must pronounce against

†From: *Foreign Relations, 1918: Russia,* vol. 2, pp. 67-68.

Germany's invasion of Russia, which she attempts to justify on the pretext of restoring order. And it is the judgment of the Government of the United States, uttered with the utmost respect, that, even with such assurances given, they could in the same way be discredited by those whose interest it was to discredit them; that a hot resentment would be generated in Russia itself, and that the whole action might play into the hands of the enemies of Russia, and particularly of the enemies of the Russian revolution, for which the Government of the United States entertains the greatest sympathy, in spite of all the unhappiness and misfortune which has for the time being sprung out of it. The Government of the united States begs once more to express to the Government of Japan its warmest friendship and confidence and once more begs it to accept these expressions of judgment as uttered only in the frankness of friendship.

POLK

24

Watchful Waiting–By Economic Support

Reinsch's telegrams from China were a great help to Wilson in deciding on his course of action in Russia. The ambassador's suggestion that economic aid would be more practicable than military support was just the answer Wilson was looking for in response to Allied pressure. And what military aid he did recommend was on the order of a force to protect the railway. Other matters, Reinsch seemed confident, would take care of themselves. Of course, those "other matters" concerned Lenin and Trotsky very much, as they viewed the situation from European Russia.

Document†

The Minister in China (Reinsch) to the Secretary of State

[Telegram]

Peking, *April 10, 1918, 5 p.m.*
[*Received 8.53 p.m.*]

Referring to my cable of April 8, 6 p.m. The American Government in holding back in the matter of intervention in Siberia is [justified] by recent reports from there, particularly British military attaché and Major Fitzwilliam, British Army. Following is a summary of the situation as it appears from here:

There is no evidence of a concerted plan on the part of Germans to control Siberia through the prisoners nor could such an attempt succeed. Earlier reports about armed prisoners were exaggerated; most of these reports came from one source in Irkutsk. A great many Austrian prisoners have become international socialists, joined Bolsheviks and thrown in their lot with Russians. Most German prisoners desire to return to Europe. In case of need Bolsheviks will make use of the technical knowledge of German officers, but the latter could not control unless the Russian people should be driven into the arms of Germany through some fatal mistake.

Intervention can do good only if understood and supported by the [omission] from there. Intervention in support of a group superimposed from above would badly upset things for the Allies. Semenov has no backing in Russia though at present [omission] by Kuroki, Japanese

†From: *Foreign Relations, 1918: Russian*, vol. 2, pp. 117-18.

officer. Any advance would put him in a helpless condition dependent entirely upon outside force. Extent of Ussuri Cossack organization not known here but other Cossacks generally stand with the workmen. Only reactionaries want intervention at all costs even in the last resort by Japan alone. The so-called Siberian autonomous government organized at Tomsk, members of which addressed President Wilson from Vladivostok by telegraph April 6, might possibly get sufficient backing in Siberia to warrant Allied support.

It is believed that the Allies, particularly the United States, still have it in their power to take action which will save Russia and Siberia from German dominion and keep up spirit of other Slavic nationalities in Europe; economic rather than military action will now accomplish this. Russian population needs clothes and manufactured goods; workmen need food held by peasants. The immediate creation of a Russian trading corporation, backed by the governments, which would import needed goods from the United States and Japan and would exchange for grain and supply same in cities, all through local Russian and Siberian committees, absolutely on condition that order be first restored so that beneficial use of materials assured—this policy if announced to people will gain their immediate adhesion. Restoration of railway traffic policing by local guards with only potential support by international force. If the policy of economic support to Siberia and restoration of traffic is put in the foreground, it is believed that other matters will take care of themselves. Should intervention come first there is danger that it will be understood to be in favor of reaction and capitalism and will alienate the people permanently. The financial support required for the economic program would be much smaller than military action would require; it would give far greater assurance of ultimate effective military action against Germany. Economic support as primary action, military assistance in the background made effective where local anarchy requires, would appear safe policy.

25

Wilson Seeks an Alternative

Negative watchful waiting was not only unendurable for America's allies, but was getting Wilson down, too. There is an interesting parallel between Trotsky's impatience with the delay in the world revolution and Wilson's feeling that he must do *something* about the Bolsheviks before it was too late, if only to save his peace program and the spirit of liberalism which, he feared, was being crushed between radicalism and reaction.

Document†

The Secretary of State to the Allied Ambassadors
AIDE—MÉMOIRE

The whole heart of the people of the United States is in the winning of this war. The controlling purpose of the Government of the United States is to do everything that is necessary and effective to win it. It wishes to cooperate in every practicable way with the Allied Governments, and to cooperate ungrudgingly; for it has no ends of its own to serve and believes that the war can be won only by common counsel and intimate concert of action. It has sought to study every proposed policy or action in which its cooperation has been asked in this spirit, and states the following conclusions in the confidence that, if it finds itself obliged to decline participation in any undertaking or course of action, it will be understood that it does so only because it deems itself precluded from participating by imperative considerations either of policy or of fact.

In full agreement with the Allied Governments and upon the unanimous advice of the Supreme War Council, the Government of the United States adopted, upon its entrance into the war, a plan for taking part in the fighting on the western front into which all its resources of men and material were to be put, and put as rapidly as possible, and it has carried out that plan with energy and success, pressing its execution more and more rapidly forward and literally putting into it the entire energy and executive force of the nation. This was its response, its very willing and hearty response, to what was the unhesitating judgment alike of its own military advisers and of the advisers of the Allied Governments. It is now considering, at the suggestion of the Supreme War Council, the possibility of making very considerable additions even to this immense program which,

†From: *Foreign Relations, 1918: Russia*, vol. 2, pp. 287-90.

if they should prove feasible at all, will tax the industrial processes of the United States and the shipping facilities of the whole group of associated nations to the utmost. It has thus concentrated all its plans and all its resources upon this single absolutely necessary object.

In such circumstances it feels it to be its duty to say that it cannot, so long as the military situation on the western front remains critical, consent to break or slacken the force of its present effort by diverting any part of its military force to other points or objectives. The United States is at a great distance from the field of action on the western front; it is at a much greater distance from any other field of action. The instrumentalities by which it is to handle its armies and its stores have at great cost and with great difficulty been created in France. They do not exist elsewhere. It is practicable for her to do a great deal in France; it is not practicable for her to do anything of importance or on a large scale upon any other field. The American Government, therefore, very respectfully requests its associates to accept its deliberate judgment that it should not dissipate its force by attempting important operations elsewhere.

It regards the Italian front as closely coordinated with the western front, however, and is willing to divert a portion of its military forces from France to Italy if it is the judgment and wish of the Supreme Command that it should do so. It wishes to defer to the decision of the Commander in Chief in this matter, as it would wish to defer in all others, particularly because it considers these two fronts so closely related as to be practically but separate parts of a single line and because it would be necessary that any American troops sent to Italy should be subtracted from the number used in France and be actually transported across French territory from the ports now used by the armies of the United States.

It is the clear and fixed judgment of the Government of the United States, arrived at after repeated and very searching reconsiderations of the whole situation in Russia, that military intervention there would add to the present sad confusion in Russia rather than cure it, injure her rather than help her, and that it would be of no advantage in the prosecution of our main design, to win the war against Germany. It can not, therefore, take part in such intervention or sanction it in principle. Military intervention would, in its judgment, even supposing it to be efficacious in its immediate avowed object of delivering an attack upon Germany from the east, be merely a method of making use of Russia, not a method of serving her. Her people could not profit by it, if they profited by it at all, in time to save them from their present distresses, and their substance would be used to maintain foreign armies, not to reconstitute their own. Military action is admissible in Russia, as the Government of the United States sees the circumstances, only to help the Czecho-Slovaks consolidate their forces and get into successful cooperation with their Slavic kinsmen and to steady any efforts at self-government or self-defense in which the Russians themselves may be willing to accept assistance. Whether from Vladivostok or from Murmansk and Archangel, the only legitimate object for which American or

Allied troops can be employed, it submits, is to guard military stores which may subsequently be needed by Russian forces and to render such aid as may be acceptable to the Russians in the organization of their own self-defense. For helping the Czecho-Slovaks there is immediate necessity and sufficient justification. Recent developments have made it evident that that it is in the interest of what the Russian people themselves desire, and the Government of the United States is glad to contribute the small force at its disposal for that purpose. It yields, also, to the judgment of the Supreme Command in the matter of establishing a small force at Murmansk, to guard the military stores at Kola, and to make it safe for Russian forces to come together in organized bodies in the north. But it owes it to frank counsel to say that it can go no further than these modest and experimental plans. It is not in a position, and has no expectation of being in a position, to take part in organized intervention in adequate force from either Vladivostok or Murmansk and Archangel. It feels that it ought to add, also, that it will feel at liberty to use the few troops it can spare only for the purposes here stated and shall feel obliged to withdraw those forces, in order to add them to the forces at the western front, if the plans in whose execution it is now intended that they should cooperate should develop into others inconsistent with the policy to which the Government of the United States feels constrained to restrict itself.

At the same time the Government of the United States wishes to say with the utmost cordiality and good will that none of the conclusions here stated is meant to wear the least color of criticism of what the other governments associated against Germany may think it wise to undertake. It wishes in no way to embarass their choices of policy. All that is intended here is a perfectly frank and definite statement of the policy which the United States feels obliged to adopt for herself and in the use of her own military forces. The Government of the United States does not wish it to be understood that in so restricting its own activities it is seeking, even by implication, to set limits to the action or to define the policies of its associates.

It hopes to carry out the plans for safeguarding the rear of the Czecho-Slovaks operating from Vladivostok in a way that will place it and keep it in close cooperation with a small military force like its own from Japan, and if necessary from the other Allies, and that will assure it of the cordial accord of all the Allied powers; and it proposes to ask all associatdd in this course of action to unite in assuring the people of Russia in the most public and solemn manner that none of the governments uniting in action either in Siberia or in northern Russia contemplates any interference of any kind with the political sovereignty of Russia, any intervention in her internal affairs, or any impairment of her territorial integrity either now or hereafter, but that each of the associated powers has the single object of affording such aid as shall be acceptable, and only such aid as shall be acceptable, to the Russian people in their endeavor to regain control of their own affairs, their own territory, and their own destiny.

It is the hope and purpose of the Government of the United States to take advantage of the earliest opportunity to send to Siberia a commission of merchants, agricultural experts, labor advisers, Red Cross representatives, and agents of the Young Men's Christian Association accustomed to organizing the best methods of spreading useful information and rendering educational help of a modest sort, in order in some systematic manner to relieve the immediate economic necessities of the people there in every way for which opportunity may open. The execution of this plan will follow and will not be permitted to embarass the military assistance rendered in the rear of the westward-moving forces of the Czecho-Slovaks.

Washington, *July 17, 1918.*

26

Lenin on Japan

Lenin's reaction to the declared Allied purpose in sending Japanese troops to Siberia was not far off the mark. However much they talked about countering German influence or reestablishing the Eastern Front, it was clear that the Allies and America could accomplish that end only by overcoming Bolshevik opposition. In this instance, Lenin is referring to a speech by Foreign Secretary Arthur Balfour explaining the intervention to the British people.

Document†

One of the weakest spots in Balfour's speech is the statement that the Japanese are going to help the Russians. *Which Russians?* In Russia today there is one power, which by its nature is destined to wage a life and death struggle against the attacks of international Imperialism—that is the power of the Soviets. The first step, however, of those Russians whom the Japanese intend to "help" as soon as they heard rumours of the advance of the latter, was to demand the abolition of the Soviet Power. Should the Japanese move into Siberia, these same "Russians" whom the Japanese are going to help will demand the abolition of the Soviets throughout the whole of Siberia. What can take the place of the Soviet Power? The only power that can take its place is a bourgeois government. But the bourgeoisie in Russia has proved clearly enough that it can only remain in power with foreign help. If a bourgeois government, supported by outside help, should establish itself in Siberia and Eastern Russia become lost to the Soviet, then in Western Russia the Soviet Power would become weakened to such an extent that it could hardly hold out for long; it would be followed by a bourgeois government, which would also need foreign help. The power to give this help would, of course, not be England. It is easy to understand what avenues are opened up by this possibility.

†From: Lenin to Arthur Ransome, June 23, 1918, in R.H. Bruce Lockhart, *British Agent* (New York: Putnams, 1933), p. 269.

27

The Open Door in Russia

Casting about for a justification for American policy in Siberia, Wilson hit upon the traditional open door policy in China. These exchanges between Paris and Washington reveal how difficult Wilson found it to explain his Russian policy to congressional critics, and why he finally dropped the idea. Meanwhile, he was being battered with demands for a full-scale military intervention by the French at Versailles.

Document†

The Commission to Negotiate Peace to the Acting Secretary of State

Paris, *January 31, 1919, 8 p.m.*
[Received February 1, 6:30 p.m.]

521. Department's 391, dated January 24th, 3 p.m. and Department's 392, January 24th, 4 p.m.

The substance of these cables has received the careful consideration of Secretary Lansing and McCormick and the latter has discussed the matter generally [*fully*] with the President who approves and authorizes the following procedure:

You are requested to ask for a second [*secret*] hearing before such committee or committees in Congress as you think best. At this hearing you will state that it is the President's wish that the Siberian situation and the activities of the administration in relation thereto be made known fully and frankly, though in strict confidence, to the members of these committees. You will then develop the strategic importance both from the point of view of Russia and of the United States of the Trans-Siberian Railway as being a principal means of access to and from the Russian people and as affording an opportunity for economic aid to Siberia where the people are relatively friendly and resistant to Bolshevik influence and where there are large bodies of Czech-Slovaks who rely upon our support as well as large numbers of enemy prisoners of war whose activities must be watched and in all cases [*if necessary*] controlled. The potential value of this railroad as a means for developing American commerce particularly

†From: U.S., Department of State, *Papers Relating to the Foreign Relations of the United States, 1919: Russia* (Washington, D.C.: Government Printing Office, 1937), pp. 246-51.

from the west coast of the United States to Russia might be mentioned. You may then narrate in considerable detail the difficulties which we have had with Japan with reference to this railway and in particular the action of Japan in practically seizing the Chinese Eastern Railway, thereby in effect controlling all intercourse to and from Russia via the Pacific. You might mention the number of troops sent by Japan for the purpose and point out that such number was far in excess of that contemplated by the arrangement under which troops of the Associated Governments were landed in Siberia. The nature of the activities of Japan including disposition of their troops and Japanese commercial activities should then be referred to [followed by] a statement of the efforts of the Government of the United States to restore the railroad to a condition where it would not be exclusively dominated by any one power.... The conversations of the President and Secretary of State with the Japanese Ambassador, the negotiations of Ambassador Morris under instructions from the Department and the economic pressure applied by the War Trade Board may be referred to. You should then describe the successful conclusion of these efforts of the United States as evidenced by the arrangements for administration of the railway by Stevens as a Russian employee and the withdrawal of substantial numbers of Japanese troops. We feel that these proceedings and their conclusion can properly be described as a very important and constructive achievement which may be of inestimable value to the people of Russia and to the United States as well as the world in general, provided they are followed through, thereby giving practical effect to the principle of the open door. You will then point out that in order to give substance and permanence to the arrangement which has been reached, it will be necessary to devise a plan for the financing of the railway and that it is the view of the President that this financing should be regarded as a joint obligation of the interested Governments and that the President is prepared to propose [and endeavor] to secure agreement on such a plan [provided] it seems probable that Congress will be prepared to appropriate the funds necessary to permit the Government of the United States to deposit [carry out] its proportional share of any financing agreed to. You may add that if the disposition of the committees whom you will be addressing is favorable to such a plan, the President will as a provisional measure and as (indicated?) in Am[erican] mission 376, January 21st, arrange through the Russian Bureau, Incorporated, or through his special fund, for a limited temporary advance to support Stevens, pending the submission to Congress of a definite financial plan provided one can be agreed to. The consequence of failure to support Stevens, as indicated by Department's 130 [113] January 6th, should be developed and the responsibility of Congress in connection therewith made clear. It is felt that it may be desirable that Woolley appear with you and state to the members of the committees the purposes and activities of the War Trade Board Russian Bureau, Incorporated, pointing out that these purposes and activities have from time to time been publicly announced and that the corporation does not constitute a secret instrumentality.

The foregoing is designed to indicate the spirit in which the President wishes the Siberian situation to be handled and you should not consider yourself bound to follow literally the suggestions made. It is desired that you treat the matter with the utmost frankness, giving all information at your disposal under, of course, a pledge of confidence.

It is desired that you cable as promptly as possible the attitude of the Congressional Committees and pending our hearing from you on this subject you are requested to hold in abeyance the giving of instructions to General Graves and the advance of money by the War Trade Board Corporation as suggested by Am[erican] mission 376, January 21.

We feel that it may be a wise practice to take Congress more into confidence on such matters and we at least desire to make the experiment in this case.

Lansing Am[erican] Mission

The Acting Secretary of State to the Commission to Negotiate Peace

Washington, *February 4, 1919, 6 p.m.*

568. For the Secretary of State and McCormick:

Your 521 January 31st, 8 p.m. I have given the suggestion made by you most careful consideration, have taken advice of the men in the Department, and then brought the question up at Cabinet today. Everyone is of the same mind that it would be very inadvisable for me to go to Congress at this time with any plan, one, of acquiring money to be expended abroad, or two, having anything to do with Russia. In regard to the first objection, having just been through the fight to obtain the money for the $100,000,000 fund for feeding Europe, I am convinced that I would not be given any consideration whatever, in view of the fact our plans in regard to the railroad—as to who are to contribute and how much it would cost—are so absolutely indefinite. In the Committee on Appropriations the whole fight made on the Food Bill by the opponents and the criticisms made even by our friends was that they did not have information enough. The information in the case of the Food Bill was so much more than anything I could offer at present, I am advised by everyone that an attempt to get any agreement from committee would be hopeless.

In regard to the second objection, the first question to be asked would be what is the Russian policy. If no answer could be given, the reasons for not being able to give an answer would have no weight. Senator Johnson is demanding that troops be withdrawn from Archangel, and there is considerable support of his position on the ground that our men are being killed and no one knows why they are still there. Of course these criticisms are unjust, but they carry more or less weight. Any attempt to commit Congress to a definite policy on the Siberian railroad, which is only a part of the whole Russian problem, would be hopeless unless some definite information could be given them on the whole subject. The Vice President said that if the Russian question were thrown into Congress at this time, it would probably jeopardize all the appropriation bills.

In view of the unanimous opinion of all who have been consulted, I think it would be wiser for me not to approach them for money for this purpose. It seems to me that it has to be settled now whether we will accept the compromise arrangement for operating railroad and then take our chance later on of being able to get Congress to assume the responsibility. If Congress then refuses to accept a carefully worked out plan that shows how much money will be required and how much each Government will contribute, then the responsibility will be on Congress, but to get Congress to commit itself to any proposal for financing the railroad—in its present mood when it is badly frightened over the amount of money we are spending and when it is so completely at sea as to what should be done in Russia—would be hopeless.

Shall I give formal approval. Japanese pressing for answer.

Polk

The Commission to Negotiate Peace to the Acting Secretary of State

Paris, February 9, 1919, 6 p.m.
[Received 11:10 p.m.]

658. From Lansing and McCormick.

Department's 568, February 4, 6 p.m. In view of situation which you report the President withdraws the suggestion with reference to presenting to congressional committees our proposed action with reference to Siberian railways. The President further authorizes the following:

1. That you formally accept the plan on behalf of the United States, with reservation as to financial responsibility which shall be the subject of further discussion, and that you notify the Japanese in this sense.
2. That you request Secretary Baker to see that instructions are given General Graves as contemplated by plan.
3. That the War Trade Board Russian Bureau, Incorporated, advance such funds as it can spare in amounts approved by the Department for the temporary support of Stevens as proposed in Mission 521, January 31st, 8 p.m.
4. That you give immediate instructions to Ambassador Morris to inaugurate negotiations for a definite plan for operating the railroad.

While in deference to your views and those of the Cabinet, the President withdraws his suggestion as to placing this matter frankly before Congress, it is desired that you keep this possibility in mind and avail of any opportunity which may seem to you to be appropriate to keep Congress advised as to our policy with reference to the Siberian railroad. It is felt that this matter can be treated entirely apart from the general Russian problem, as, irrespective of what our policy may be toward Russia, and irrespective of further [*future*] Russian developments, it is essential that we maintain the policy of the open door with reference to the Siberian and particularly the Chinese Eastern Railway. This cable has been seen and approved by the President.

Am[erican] Mission

28

The Military Opinion

From the outset the American military was never enthusiastic about Siberia. Wilson knew about these feelings, and the reasons for them, from letters like this one from General Graves to the Adjutant General. It was another factor he had to take into account at Versailles in his search for a new way to implement watchful waiting.

Document†

The situation here as I see it merits careful consideration. Conditions in Siberia are growing worse daily. General Horvat, a typical reactionary, supported by the Russian Army Officer Class, has been appointed by the Omsk Government representative in eastern Siberia. This crowd if not in favor of a monarchy are certainly in favor of some form of autocratic government. This is well known to and opposed by the great majority of Russians. The opinion just now is that this crowd could not remain in power 24 hours in eastern Siberia after allied troops are removed. As I see the situation they know the poorer classes will not attack them as long as allied troops are here and they are utilizing to the fullest extent this time to entrench themselves, get together a military force which they hope will be strong enough to hold them in power when allied troops are removed. I think some blood will be shed when troops move out but the longer we stay the greater will be the bloodshed when allied troops do go, as in effect each day we remain here, now that war with Germany is over, we are by our mere presence helping establish a form of autocratic government which the people of Siberia will not stand for and our stay is creating some feeling against the allied governments because of the effect it has. The classes seem to be growing wider apart and the feeling between them more bitter daily.

---

†From: Graves to Secretary of War, November 22, 1918, Papers of Woodrow Wilson, Library of Congress, Washington, D.C.

29

The Versailles Conference

At one of the early meetings of the Versailles Conference, the Big Four wrestled with the Bolshevik problem and the issue of who or what should represent the legitimate Russian government. Wilson's deepening understanding of the dimensions of the problem brought him closer in line with Prime Minister Lloyd George, but he was still primarily concerned with dividing the Russian people from the Bolsheviki and, if possible, dealing with each on a separate basis. Increasingly, he would be absorbed in the task of "containing" the Bolsheviks in Russia, where he was sure they would burn themselves out.

Document†

Mr. Lloyd George commenced his statement setting forth the information in the possession of the British Government regarding the Russian situation, by referring to the matter which had been exposed recently in *L'Humanité*. He stated that he wished to point out that there had been a serious misconception on the part of the French Government as to the character of the proposal of the British Government. The British proposal did not contemplate in any sense whatsoever, a recognition of the Bolsheviki Government, nor a suggestion that Bolshevik delegates be invited to attend the Conference. The British proposal was to invite all of the different governments now at war within what used to be the Russian Empire, to a truce of God, to stop reprisals and outrages and to send men here to give, so to speak, an account of themselves. The Great Powers would then try to find a way to bring some order out of chaos. These men were not to be delegates to the Peace Conference, and he agreed with the French Government entirely that they should not be made members of the Conference.

Mr. Lloyd George then proceeded to set forth briefly the reasons which had led the British Government to make this proposal. They were as follows:

Firstly, the real facts are not known;

Secondly, if it is impossible to get the facts, the only way is to adjudicate the question; and

†From: "Notes on Conversations Held in the Office of M. Pichon at the Quai d'Orsay, January 16, 1919," in U.S., Department of State, *Papers Relating to the Foreign Relations of the United States: The Paris Peace Conference, 1919*, (Washington, D.C.: Government Printing Office, 1943), vol. 3, pp. 588-93.

Thirdly, conditions in Russia are very bad; there is general mis-government and starvation. It is not known who is obtaining the upper hand, but the hope that the Bolshevik Government would collapse has not been realized. In fact, there is one report that the Bolsheviki are stronger than ever, that their internal position is strong, and that their hold on the people is stronger. Take, for instance, the case of the Ukraine. Some adventurer raises a few men and overthrows the government. The government is incapable of overthrowing him. It is also reported that the peasants are becoming Bolsheviki. It is hardly the business of the Great Powers to intervene either in lending financial support to one side or the other, or in sending munitions to either side.

Mr. Lloyd George stated that there seemed to be three possible policies:

1. Military intervention. It is true that the Bolsheviki movement is as dangerous to civilization as German militarism, but as to putting it down by the sword, is there anyone who proposes it? It would mean holding a certain number of vast provinces in Russia. The Germans with one million men on their Eastern Front only held the fringe of this territory. If he now proposed to send a thousand British troops to Russia for that purpose, the armies would mutiny. The same applies to U.S. troops in Siberia; also to Canadians and French as well. The mere idea of crushing Bolshevism by a military force is pure madness. Even admitting that it is done, who is to occupy Russia? No one can conceive or undertake to bring about order by force.

2. A cordon. The second suggestion is to besiege Bolshevik Russia. Mr. Lloyd George wondered if those present realized what this would mean. From the information furnished him Bolshevik Russia has no corn, but within this territory there are 150,000,000 men, women and children. There is now starvation in Petrograd and Moscow. This is not a health cordon; it is a death cordon. Moreover, as a matter of fact, the people who would die are just the people that the Allies desire to protect. It would not result in the starvation of the Bolsheviki; it would simply mean the death of our friends. The cordon policy is a policy which, as humane people, those present could not consider.

Mr. Lloyd George asked, who was there to overthrow the Bolsheviki? He had been told there were three men, Denikin, Kolchak and Knox. In considering the chances of these people to overthrow the Bolsheviki, he pointed out that he had received information that the Czecho-Slovaks now refused to fight; that the Russian Army was not to be trusted, and that while it was true that a Bolshevik Army had recently gone over to Kolchak it was never certain that just the reverse of this did not take place. If the Allies counted on any of these men, he believed they were building on quick-sand. He had heard a lot of talk about Denikin, but when he looked on the map he found that Denikin was occupying a little backyard near the Black Sea. Then he had been told that Denikin had recognized Kolchak, but when he looked on the map there was a great solid block of territory between Denikin and Kolchak. Moreover, from information received it would appear that kolchak has been collecting members of the old regime around him, and would seem to be at heart a monarchist. It appeared that the Czecho-Slovaks were finding this out. The sympathies of the Czecho-Slovaks are very democratic, and they are not at all prepared to fight for the restoration of the old conditions in Russia.

Mr. Lloyd George stated that he was informed that at the present time two-thirds of Bolshevik Russia was starving.

Institutions of Bolsheviki are institutions of old Czarist regime. This is not what one would call creating a new world.

3. The third alternative was contained in the British proposal, which was to summon these people to Paris to appear before those present, somewhat in the way that the Roman Empire summoned chiefs of outlying tributary states to render an account of their actions.

Mr. Lloyd George pointed out the fact that the argument might be used that there were already here certain representatives of these Governments; but take, for instance, the case of Sassonoff, who claims to represent the Government of Omsk. As a matter of fact, Sassonoff cannot speak from personal observation. He is nothing but a partisan, like all the rest. He has never been in contact, and is not now in direct contact with the Government at Omsk.

It would be manifestly absurd for those who are responsible for bringing about the Peace Conference, to come to any agreement and leave Paris when one-half of Europe and one-half of Asia is still in flames. Those present must settle this question or make fools of themselves.

Mr. Lloyd George referred to the objection that had been raised to permitting Bolshevik delegates to come to Paris. It had been claimed that they would convert France and England to Bolshevism. If England becomes Bolshevist, it will not be because a single Bolshevist representative is permitted to enter England. On the other hand, if a military enterprise were started against the Bolsheviki, that would make England Bolshevist, and there would be Soviet in London. For his part, Mr. Lloyd George was not afraid of Bolshevism if the facts are known in England and the United States. The same applies to Germany. He was convinced that an educated democracy can be always trusted to turn down Bolshevism.

Under all the circumstances, Mr. Lloyd George saw no better way out than to follow the third alternative. Let the Great Powers impose their conditions and summon these people to Paris to given an account of themselves to the Great Powers, not to the Peace Conference.

M. Pichon suggested that it might be well to ask M. Noulens, the French Ambassador to Russia, who had just returned to France, to appear before the meeting tomorrow morning, and give those present his views on the Russian situation.

President Wilson stated that he did not see how it was possible to controvert the statement of Mr. Lloyd George. He thought that there was a force behind his discussion which was no doubt in his mind, but which it might be desirable to bring out a little more definitely. He did not believe that there would be sympathy anywhere with the brutal aspect of Bolshevism. If it were not for the fact of the domination of large vested interests in the political and economic world, while it might be true that this evil was in process of discussion and slow reform, it must be admitted, that the general body of men have grown impatient at the failure to bring about the necessary reform. He stated that there were many men who represented large vested interests in the United States who saw the necessity for these reforms and desired something which should be worked out at the Peace Conference, namely, the establishment of some machinery to provide for the opportunity of the individuals greater than the world has ever known. Capital and labor in the United States are not friends. Still they are not enemies in the sense that they are thinking of resorting to physical force to settle their differences. But they are distrustful, each of the other. Society cannot go on on that plane. On the one hand, there is a minority possessing capital and brains; on the other, a majority consisting of the great bodies of workers who are essential to the minority, but do not trust the minority, and feel that the minority will never render them their rights. A way must be found to put trust and cooperation between these two.

President Wilson pointed out that the whole world was disturbed by this question beofre the Bolsheviki came into power. Seeds need soil, and the Bolsheviki seeks found the soil already prepared for them.

President Wilson stated that he would not be surprised to find that the reaosn why British and United States troops would not be ready to enter Russia to fight the Bolsheviki was explained by the fact that the troops were not at all sure that if they put down Bolshevism they would not bring about a re-establishment of the ancient order. For example, in making a speech recently, to a well-dressed audience in New York City who were not to be expected to show such feeling, Mr. Wilson had referred casually to Russia, stating that the United States would do its utmost to aid her suppressed people. The audience exhibited the greatest enthusiasm, and this had remained in the President's mind as an index to where the sympathies of the New World are.

President Wilson believed that those present would be playing against the principle of free spirit of the world if they did not give Russia a chance to find herself along the lines of utter freedom. He concurred with Mr. Lloyd George's view and supported his recommendations that the third line of procedure be adopted.

President Wilson stated that he had also, like Mr. Lloyd George, received a memorandum from his experts which agreed substantially with the information which Mr. Lloyd George had received. There was one point which he thought particularly worthy of notice, and that was the report that the strength of the Bolshevik leaders lay in the argument that if they were not supported by the people of Russia, there would be foreign intervention, and the Bolsheviki were the only thing that stood between the Russians and foreign military control. It might well be that if the

Bolsheviki were assured that they were safe from foreign aggression, they might lose support of their own movement.

President Wilson further stated that he understood that the danger of destruction of all hope in the Baltic provinces was immediate, and that it should be made very clear if the British proposal were adopted, that the Bolsheviki would have to withdraw entirely from Lithuania and Poland. If they would agree to this to refrain from reprisals and outrages, he, for his part, would be prepared to receive representatives from as many groups and centers of action, as chose to come, and endeavor to assist them to reach a solution of their problem.

He thought that the British proposal contained the only suggestions that led anywhere. It might lead nowhere. But this could at least be found out.

M. Pichon referred again to the suggestion that Ambassador Noulens be called before the meeting.

Mr. Balfour suggested that it might be well to call the Dutch Consul, lately in Petrograd, if it was the desire of those present to hear the anti-Bolshevik side.

Baron Sonnino suggested that M. Scavenius, Minister of Denmark, recently in Russia, would be able to give interesting data on the Russian situation.

Those present seemed to think that it might be desirable to hear what these gentlemen might have to say.

30

Hoover's Advice

Herbert Hoover's lengthy memorandum sums up what Wilson and the American Mission at Versailles finally agreed could and could not be done about Bolshevism. Wilson's diplomatic moral embargo on Russia combined with a food relief program was the eventual result.

Document†

As the result of Bolshevik economic conceptions the people of Russia are dying of hunger and disease at the rate of some hundreds of thousands monthly in a country that formerly supplied food to a large part of the world.

I feel it is my duty to lay before you in just as few words as possible my views as to the American relation to Bolshevism and its manifestations. These views at least have the merit of being an analysis of information and thought gleaned from my own experience and the independent sources which I now have over the whole of Europe, through our widespread relief organization.

It simply cannot be denied that this swinging of the social pendulum from the tyranny of the extreme right to the tyranny of the extreme left is based on a foundation of real social grievance. The tyranny of the reactionaries in Eastern and Central Europe for generations before the war, and the suffering of their common people is but a commonplace to every social student. This situation was thrown into bold relief by the war and the breakdown of these reactionary tyrannies. After fighting actually stopped on the various fronts the famine which followed has further emphasized the gulf between the lower and upper classes. The poor were starved and driven mad in the presence of extravagance and waste.

It is to be noticed that the Bolshevik ascendancy or even their strong attempts so far are confined to areas of former reactionary tyranny. Their courses represent the not unnatural violence of a mass of ignorant humanity, who themselves have learned in grief of tyranny and violence over generations. Our people, who enjoy so great liberty and general comfort, cannot fail to sympathize to some degree with these blind gropings for better social condition. If former revolutions in ignorant masses are any guide, the pendulum will yet swing back to some moderate position when bitter experience has taught the economic and social follies

†From: Hoover to Wilson, March 28, 1919, Papers of Edward M. House, Sterling Library, Yale University, New Haven, Conn., as reprinted in Arno J. Mayer, *Politics and Diplomacy of Peacemaking* (N.Y.: Alfred Knopf, 1967), pp. 474-78.

of present obsessions. No greater fortune can come to the world than that these foolish ideas should have an opportunity somewhere of bankrupting themselves.

It is not necessary for any American to debate the utter foolishness of these economic tenets. We must all agree that our processes of production and distribution, the outgrowth of a hundred generations, in the stimulation to individual initiative, the large equality of opportunity and infinite development of mind and body, while not perfect, come about as near perfection as is possible from the mixture of avarice, ambition, altruism, intelligence, ignorance and education, of which the human animal is today composed. The Bolshevik's land of illusion is that he can perfect these human qualities by destroying the basic processes of production and distribution instead of devoting himself to securing a better application of the collective surplus.

Politically, the Bolsheviki most certainly represent a minority in every country where they are in control, and as such they constitute a tyranny that is the negation of democracy, for democracy as I see it must rest on the execution of the will of the majority expressed by free and unterrified suffrage. As a tyranny, the Bolshevik has resorted to terror, bloodshed and murder to a degree long since abandoned even amongst reactionary tyrannies.

He has even to a greater degree relied upon criminal instinct to support his doctrines than even autocracy did. By enveloping into his doctrines the cry of the helpless and the downtrodden, he has embraced a large degree of emotionalism and has thereby given an impulse to his propaganda comparable only to the impulse of large spiritual movements. This propaganda, however, in my view will stir other populations only in ratio to their proportions of the suffering and ignorant and criminal. I feel myself, therefore, that the political danger of spread of Bolshevism by propaganda is a direct factor of the social and political development of the population which they attempt to impregnate. Where the gulf between the middle classes and the lower classes is large, and where the lower classes have been kept in ignorance and distress, this propaganda will be fatal and do violence to normal democratic development. For these reasons, I have no fear of it in the United States, and my fears as to other countries would be gauged by the above criterion. It is possible that the Soviet type of government might take hold in some other countries as a primitive form of democracy, but its virulence will be tempered by their previous degree of political subversion.

There remains in my mind one more point to be examined, that is as to whether the Bolshevik centers now stirred by great emotional hopes will not undertake large military crusades in an attempt to impose their doctrines on other defenseless people. This is a point on which my mind is divided with the evidence at hand, and it seems to me that the whole treatment of the problem must revolve on the determination of this one question. If this spirit is inherent in their doctrine, it appears to me that we must disregard all other questions and be prepared to fight, for exactly the same reasons that we entered the European War against Germany. If this is not the case, then it appears to me that from an American point of view we should not involve ourselves in what may be a ten year military entanglement in Europe. The American people cannot say that we are going to insist that any given population must work out its internal social problems according to our particular conception of democracy. In any event, I have the most serious doubt that outside forces entering upon such an enterprise can do other than infinite harm, for any great wave of emotion must ferment and spread under repression. In the swing of the social pendulum from the extreme left back toward the right, it will find the point of stabilization based on racial instincts that could never be established by outside intervention.

I think we have also to contemplate what would actually happen if we undertook military intervention in, say, a case like Hungary. We should probably be involved in years of police duty, and our first act would probably in the nature of things make us a party of reestablishing the reactionary classes in their economic domination over the lower classes. This is against our fundamental national spirit, and I doubt whether our soldiers under these circumstances could resist infection with Bolshevik ideas. It also requires consideration as to whether or not our people at home, on gradual enlightenment as to the social wrongs of the lower classes in these countries, would stand for our providing power by which such reactionaries held their position, and we would perchance be thrown into an attempt as governors to work out some social reorganization of these countries. We thus become a mandatory with a vengeance. We become, in fact, one of four mandatories, each with a different political and social outlook, for it would necessarily be a joint Allied undertaking. Furthermore, in our present engagements with France, England and Italy, we become a junior in this partnership of four. It is therefore inevitable that in these matters where our views and principles are at variance with the European Allies we would find ourselves subordinated and even committed to policies against our convictions.

In all these lights, I have the following three suggestions:

First: We cannot even remotely recognize this murderous tyranny without stimulating actionist radicalism in every country in Europe and without transgressing on every National ideal of our own.

Second: That some Neutral of international reputation for probity and ability should be allowed to create a second Belgian Relief Commission for Russia. He should ask the Northern Neutrals who are especially interested both politically and financially in the restoration of better conditions in Russia, to give to him diplomatic, financial and transportation support; that he should open negotiations with the Allied governments on the ground of desire to enter upon the humane work of saving life, and ask the conditions upon which ships carrying food and other necessaries will be allowed to pass. He should be told that we will raise no obstructions and would even help in his humanitarian task if he gets assurances that the Bolsheviki will cease all militant action across certain defined boundaries and cease their subsidizing of disturbances abroad; under these conditions that he could raise money, ships and food, either from inside or outside Russia; that he must secure an agreement covering equitable distribution, and he might even demand that Germany help pay for this. This plan does not involve any recognition or relationship by the Allies of the Bolshevik murderers now in control any more than England recognized germany in its deals with the Belgian Relief. It would appear to me that such a proposal would at least test out whether this is a militant force engrossed upon world domination. If such an arrangement could be accomplished it might at least give a period of rest along the frontiers of Europe and would give some hope of stabilization. Time can thus be taken to determine whether or not this whole system is a world danger, and whether the Russian people will not themselves swing back to moderation and themselves bankrupt these ideas. This plan, if successful, would save an immensity of helpless human life and would save our country from further entanglements which today threaten to pull us from our National ideals.

Third: I feel strongly the time has arrived for you again a reassert your spitirual leadership of democracy in the world as opposed to tyrannies of all kinds. Could you not take an early opportunity to analyze, as only you can, Bolshevism from its political, economic, humane and its criminal points of view, and, while yielding its aspirations, sympathetically to show its utter foolishness as a basis of economic development; show its true social ends; rap our own reactionaries for their destruction of social betterment and thereby their stimulation of Bolshevism; point, however, to the steady progress of real democracy in these roads of social betterment. I believe you would again align the hearts of the suffering for orderly progress against anarchy, not alone in Russia but in every Allied country.

If the militant features of Bolshevism were drawn in colors with their true parallel with Prussianism as an attempt at world domination that we do not stand for, it would check the fears that today haunt all men's minds.

31

Red Scare

Wilson's efforts to appropriate the red scare to secure approval of the Treaty of Versailles, and thus hasten the return of international stability, are an unpleasant aftermath to a time of troubles. They are best understood in connection with his anxiety about the League of Nations.

Document†

The Acting Secretary of State to the Counsul at Vladivostok (Caldwell)

Washington, *September 9, 1919, 6 p.m.*

In a speech at Kansas City Saturday, September 6, urging the ratification of the Peace Treaty, the President made the following allusion to the situation in Russia and the character of the Bolshevik régime:

"My fellow citizens, it does not make any difference what kind of a minority governs you, if it is a minority. And the thing we must see to is that no minority anywhere masters tne majority.

That is at the heart, my fellow citizens, of the tragical things that are happening in that great country which we long to help and can find no way that is effective to help—I mean the greal realm of Russia. The men who now are measurably in control of the affairs of Russia represent nobody but themselves. They have again and again been challenged to call a constitutional convention. They have again and again been challenged to prove that they had some kind of a mandate, even from a single class of their fellow citizens. And they dared not attempt it; they have no mandate from anybody.

There are only thirty-four of them, I am told, and there were more than thirty-four men who used to control the destinies of Europe from Wilhelmstrasse. There is a closer monopoly of power in Petrograd and Moscow than there ever was in Berlin, and the thing that is intolerable is not that the Russian people are having their way but that another group of men more cruel than the Czar himself is controlling the destinies of that great people.

And I want to say here and now that I am against the control of any minority anywhere."

Following passage, same topic, from speech delivered at Des Moines also on September 6:

"What happened in Russia was not a sudden and accidental thing. The people of Russia were maddened with the suppression of Czarism. When at last the chance came to throw off those chains, they threw them off at

†From: *Foreign Relations, 1919: Russia,* pp. 119-20.

first, with hearts full of confidence and hope and then they found out that they had been again deceived. There was no assembly chosen to frame a constitution for them, or rather there was an assembly chosen to choose a constitution for them and it was suppressed and dispersed, and a little group of men just as selfish, just as ruthless, just as pitiless as the Czar himself assumed control and exercised their power, by terror and not by right.

And in other parts of Europe the poison spread. The poison of disorder, the poison of revolt, the poison of chaos. And do you honestly think, my fellow citizens, that none of that poison has got in the veins of this free people? Do you know that the world is all now one single whispering gallery. These antennae of the wireless telegraph are the symbols of our age.

All the impulses of mankind are thrown out upon the air and reach to the ends of the earth. With the tongue of the wireless and the tongue of the telegraph all the suggestions of disorder are spread through the world. And money coming from nobody knows where is deposited in capitals like Stockholm to be used for the propaganda of disorder and discontent and dissolution throughout the world, and men look you calmly in the face in America and say that they are for that sort of revolution, when that sort of revolution means government by terror, government by force, not government by vote.

It is the negation of everything that is American, but it is spreading and so long as disorder continues, so long as the world is kept waiting for the answer of the kind of peace we are going to have and what kind of guarantees there are to be behind that peace, that poison will steadily spread, more and more rapidly until it may be that even this beloved land of ours will be distracted and distorted by it."

32

Wilson's "Final Challenge"

In his last days Wilson finally reached the conclusion that only by restoring the spirit of Christ to western capitalist civilization could it prevail against the threat of bolshevism. His questionings reflected a deep sense of discouragement at what had evolved into "normalcy" after Versailles and the fight for the league.

Document†

In these doubtful and anxious days, when all the world is at unrest and, look which way you will, the road ahead seems darkened by shadows which portend dangers of many kinds, it is only common prudence that we should look about us and attempt to assess the causes of distress and the most likely means of removing them.

There must be some real ground for the universal unrest and perturbation. It is not to be found in superficial politics or in mere economic blunders. It probably lies deep at the sources of the spiritual life of our time. It leads to revolution; and perhaps if we take the case of the Russian Revolution, the outstanding event of its kind in our age, we may find a good deal of instruction for our judgment of present critical situations and circumstances.

What gave rise to the Russian Revolution? The answer can only be that it was the product of a whole social system. It was not in fact a sudden thing. It had been gathering head for several generations. It was due to the systematic denial to the great body of Russians of the rights and privileges which all normal men desire and must have if they are to be contented and within reach of happiness. The lives of the great mass of the Russian people contained no opportunities, but were hemmed in by barriers against which they were constantly flinging their spirits, only to fall back bruised and dispirited. Only the powerful were suffered to secure their rights or even to gain access to the means of material success.

It is to be noted as a leading fact of our time that it was against 'capitalism' that the Russian leaders directed their attack. It was capitalism that made them see red; and it is against capitalism under one name or another that the discontented classes everywhere draw their indictment.

There are thoughtful and well-informed men all over the world who believe, with much apparently sound reason, that the abstract thing, the

†From: Dodd and Baker, eds., *The Public Papers of Woodrow Wilson*, vol. 6, pp. 536-39.

system, which we call capitalism is indispensable to the industrial support and development of modern civilization. And yet everyone who has an intelligent knowledge of social forces must know that great and widespread reactions like that which is now unquestionably manifesting itself against capitalism do not occur without cause or provocation; and before we commit ourselves irreconcilably to an attitude of hostility to this movement of the time, we ought frankly to put to ourselves the question, Is the capitalistic system unimpeachable? which is another way of asking, Have capitalists generally used their power for the benefit of the countries in which their capital is employed and for the benefit of their fellow men?

Is it not, on the contrary, too true that capitalists have often seemed to regard the men whom they used as mere instruments of profit, whose physical and mental powers it was legitimate to exploit with as slight cost to themselves as possible, either of money or of sympathy? Have not many fine men who were actuated by the highest principles in every other relationship of life seemed to hold that generosity and humane feeling were not among the imperative mandates of conscience in the conduct of a banking business, or in the development of an industrial or commercial enterprise?

And, if these offenses against high morality and true citizenship have been frequently observable, are we to say that the blame for the present discontent and turbulence is wholly on the side of those who are in revolt against them? Ought we not, rather, to seek a way to remove such offenses and make life itself clean for those who will share honorably and cleanly in it?

The world has been made safe for democracy. There need now be no fear that any such mad design as that entertained by the insolent and ignorant Hohenzollerns and their counselors may prevail against it. But democracy has not yet made the world safe against irrational revolution. That supreme task, which is nothing less than the salvation of civilization, now faces democracy, insistent, imperative. There is no escaping it, unless everything we have built up is presently to fall in ruin about us; and the United States, as the greatest of democracies, must undertake it.

The road that leads away from revolution is clearly marked, for it is defined by the nature of men and of organized society. It therefore behooves us to study very carefully and very candidly the exact nature of the task and the means of its accomplishment.

The nature of men and of organized society dictates the maintenance in every field of action of the highest and purest standards of justice and of right dealing; and it is essential to efficacious thinking in this critical matter that we should not entertain a narrow or technical conception of justice. By justice the lawyer generally means the prompt, fair, and open application of impartial rules; but we call ours a Christian civilization, and a Christian conception of justice must be much higher. It must include sympathy and helpfulness and a willingness to forego self-interest in order to promote and welfare, happiness, and contentment of others and of the community as a whole. This is what our age is blindly feeling after in its reaction against what it deems the too great selfishness of the capitalistic system.

The sum of the whole matter is that, that our civilization cannot survive materially unless it be redeemed spiritually. It can be saved only by becoming permeated with the spirit of Christ and being made free and happy by the practices which spring out of that spirit. Only thus can discontent be driven out and all the shadows lifted from the road ahead.

Here is the final challenge to our churches, to our political organizations, and to our capitalists—to everyone who fears God or loves his country. Shall we not earnestly coöperate to bring in the new day?

Part three

Bibliographic Essay

On the formation of Woodrow Wilson's character and world outlook there are several fine biographies. The standard work used to be Ray Stannard Baker, *Woodrow Wilson: Life and Letters*, 8 vols. (New York: Doubleday, Doran & Co., 1927-1939), which is now being replaced by Arthur S. Link's monumental *Wilson*, 5 vols. (Princeton: Princeton University Press, 1947-1965.) Professor Link has not yet reached the Russian Revolution in his study, and touches upon it only briefly in *Wilson the Diplomatist: a Look at His Major Foreign Policies* (Baltimore: Johns Hopkins, 1957). If he holds to the same position in his full-scale life of Wilson, Professor Link can be expected to elaborate on his argument that the president sent troops "only in small numbers and for the briefest time possible, as if to chaperone Allied conduct in these areas" (p. 118). Though by no means comprehensive, William Diamond's *The Economic Thought of Woodrow Wilson* (Baltimore: Johns Hopkins Press, 1943), remains the principal source for those interested in the development of Wilson's views on capitalism. An important reexamination of those views is Martin J. Sklar, "Woodrow Wilson and the Political Economy of Modern United States Liberalism," reprinted in *A New History of Leviathan: Essays on the Rise of the American Corporate State*, eds. Ronald Radosh and Murray Rothbard (New York: E.P. Dutton & Co., 1972). Sklar concludes that historians who have studied Wilson appear to "harbor guilt feelings about capitalism," but that he himself, and the "corporate and political policy-makers of the United States" in general, have had no such guilt feelings. Yet as this essay and the documents printed above suggest, Wilson did have uneasy feelings about capitalism dating back to his youth in the postbellum south, however, he remained unable to resolve these tensions and his commitment to economic expansion.

Primary reading in Wilson's writings and speeches may help the student to decide what influences the future president felt in his early days, which he carried with him in his political career, and which he discarded. The standard collection is Ray Stannard Baker and William E. Dodd eds., *The Public Papers of Woodrow Wilson*, 6 vols. (New York: Harper & Bros. 1925-1927. Once again this is being replaced by the efforts of Arthur S. Link and his associates who have been editing *The Papers of Woodrow Wilson*, 17 vols. (Princeton: Princeton University Press, 1966 - 19   ). With these (and other) materials now available, a study of Wilson's prepresidential years with an emphasis upon the problem of revolution and violent social change is both feasible and needed.

Work on Wilson's policy toward the Mexican Revolution has produced two important studies in addition to Howard F. Cline's, *The United States and Mexico* (Cambridge: Harvard University Press, 1953). They are Peter Calvert's *The Mexican Revolution, 1910-1914: The Diplomacy of Anglo-American Conflict* (Cambridge. At the University Press, 1968), and Robert Freeman Smith, *The United States and Revolutionary Nationalism in Mexico, 1916-1922* (Chicago: University of Chicago Press, 1962). Others may not find the antecedents for Wilson's reaction to the Bolshevik revolution that I have suggested in my essay here, but the value of these studies is such that they are worthwhile (if not essential) for the student of American foreign policy in this century. One should also consult the appropriate Baker and Link volumes.

For the diplomacy of the neutrality period the best place to begin is with Ernest R. May's *The World War and American Isolation* (Cambridge: Harvard University Press, 1959), but one should not stop there. Harley Notter's, *The Origins of the Foreign Policy of Woodrow Wilson* (Baltimore: Johns Hopkins Press, 1937) holds up well; but both these books should be supplemented by a more recent specialized study on the economics of alliance warfare and the problem of responsibility for the post-World War I world order, Carl Phillip Parrini's *Heir to Empire: U.S. Economic Diplomacy, 1916-1922* (Pittsburgh: University of Pittsburgh Press, 1969).

Russia's key place in the postwar outlook of United States policy makers, Wilson included, is revealed in David R. Francis, *Russia From the American Embassy* (New York: Charles Scribner's Sons, 1921).

Francis's memoirs are especially useful because they cover the 1916 prerevolutionary period when American interests in postwar Russia were chiefly commercial and the great political hopes stirred by the March revolution as well as the great disillusionment following the Bolshevik takeover. Summing up the ideological position of the Wilson administration through these rapid changes is N. Gordon Levin's *Woodrow Wilson and World Politics: America's Response to War and Revolution* (New York: Oxford University Press, 1968). A standard text such as Sidney Harcave's very readable *Russia: A History* (New York: J.P. Lippincott Company, 1953) should supply sufficient background before looking into the events of the Russian Revolution itself. In this endeavor no one is a better guide than E.H. Carr, whose volumes on *The Bolshevik Revolution 1917-1923*, New York: St. Martin's Press, 1950-1952) are likely to remain preeminent in the field for a long time indeed. Christopher Hill's brief *Lenin and the Russian Revolution* (London: Penguin Books, 1971 ed.) will not satisfy a serious student's desire to know everything about the Bolshevik leader, but the broad outlines of his thought are there. For Lenin in a broader setting, see Barrington Moore, Jr., *Soviet Politics—The Dilemma of Power* (Cambridge: Harvard University Press, 1950).

On the initial stages of the confrontation there is Arno J. Mayer's, *Wilson vs. Lenin: Political Origins of the New Diplomacy, 1917-1918* (Cleveland: World Publishing Co., 1963), which concludes that "Clemenceau eventually triumphed over both Wilson and Lenin at the Paris Peace Conference, [but] Clemenceau and his supporters at best scored a short-lived and pyrrhic victory" (p. 393). Books on the general area of Russian-American Relations between 1917 and 1921 are more than plentiful. An early study by the best-known diplomatic historian of the day is, *The Foreign Policies of Soviet Russia* (London: J.M. Dent & Sons, 1924) by Alfred L.P. Dennis. It is a surprisingly impressive of work given the materials available to Dennis and repays reading even today. Then came Louis Fischer, *The Soviets in World Affairs, A History of the Relations Between the Soviet Union and the Rest of the World 1917-1929*, 2 vols. (London: Jonathan Cape, 1930), which is a sympathetic account. In the World War II era specialized studies began appearing which added many new insights to the general picture. Among the best were John W. Wheeler-Bennett, *The Forgotten Peace (Brest-Litovsk, March 1918)*, (New York: William Morrow & Co., 1939) and Leonid I. Strakhovsky's *Intervention at Archangel: The Story of Allied Intervention and Russian Counter-Revolution in North Russia, 1918-1920* (Princeton: Princeton University Press, 1944).

Increased interest in the origins of Soviet-American difficulties stimualted several post-World War II studies, including John Albert White, *The Siberian Intervention* (Princeton: Princeton University Press, 1950, William Appleman Williams, *American-Russian Relations, 1781-1947* (New York: Rinehart & Co., 1952), Robert D. Warth, *The Allies and the Russian Revolution, From the Fall of the Monarchy to the Peace of Brest-Litovsk* (Durham, N.C.: University of North Carolina Press, 1954), Betty Miller Unterberger, *America's Siberian Expedition, 1918-1920, A Study of National Policy* (Durham: University of North Carolina Press, 1956), and the very detailed volumes by George F. Kennan, *Russia Leaves the War* (Princeton: Princeton University Press, 1956) and *The Decision to Intervene* (Princeton: Princeton University Press, 1958). In addition to finding the basic interpretations historians have given to the events of these years, one can locate nearly all the important works not listed in this bibliography in the bibliographies of these books.

Special works dealing with the Bolshevik problem at Versailles have also appeared in increasing numbers in recent years, but one should really begin the study of this area with another memoir, Herbert Hoover's, *The Ordeal of Woodrow Wilson* (New York: McGraw-Hill, 1958), which includes the key memoranda Hoover sent to the president on the best way to combat Bolshevism with food relief. Hoover comments in ending his book that Wilson would never have accepted the Soviet Union into the United Nations as he "conceived the League as an association of free nations, not to include men and dictatorships conspiring for its ruin." (p. 302.) Nor should one ignore Ray Stannard Baker's *Woodrow Wilson and World Settlement*, 3 vols. (New York: Doubleday & Co., 1922-1923), before going on to John M. Thompson, *Russia, Bolshevism, and the Versailles Peace* (Princeton: Princeton University Press, 1966) and Arno J. Mayer's massive *Politics and Diplomacy of Peacemaking: Containment and Counterrevolution at Versailles, 1918-1919* (New York: Alfred Knopf, 1967).

Ancillary works dealing with Allied policy and the Bolshevik threat include, Richard Ullman, *Anglo-Soviet Relations, 1917-1921*, 3 vols. (Princeton: Princeton University Press, 1916-1972), Piotre S. Wandycz, *France and Her Eastern Allies, 1919-1925* (Minneapolis: University of Minnesota Press, 1962) and James William Morley, *The Japanese Thrust into Siberia, 1918* (New York: Columbia University Press, 1957). For a longer perspective on the problem of recognition, see Edward M. Bennett, *Recognition of Russia: An American Foreign Policy Dilemma* (Waltham, Mass.: Balisdell Publishing Co., 1970), Robert Paul Browder, *The Origins of Soviet-American Diplomacy* (Princeton: Princeton University Press, 1953), and Beatrice Fransworth, *William C. Bullitt and the Soviet Union* (Bloomington, Indiana University Press, 1967). And for an extension into the Cold War period, see Thomas G. Paterson, ed., *Containment and the Cold War: American Foreign Policy Since 1945* (Reading, Mass.: Addison-Wesley Publishing Company, 1973).

In a final category, I should like to mention two books on "ideology" which may help the student to wrestle with the problem of ideological determination and expediency. First, the older study of *Soviet Marxism* by Herbert Marcuse (New York: Columbia University Press, 1958) and the very recent book by Joan Hoff Wilson, *Ideology and Economics: U.S. Relations with the Soviet Union, 1918-1933* (Columbia, Missouri: University of Missouri Press, 1974). I have, as suggested above, made no effort to list every book in this bibliography pertaining to Wilson and the Bolsheviks. It is intended to be a guide to further reading, not a listing for the specialist. Primary materials such as diaries, autobiographies, and printed documents and sources for manuscript materials are referred to in each of the secondary works listed and are not repeated here.